Human Rights – Disability – Children

Towards international instruments for disability rights: the special case of disabled children

Proceedings of the Conference

Organised by the Division of the Partial Agreement
in the Social and Public Health Field

under the aegis of the Norwegian chairmanship of the
Committee of Ministers

Council of Europe, Strasbourg
8-9 November 2004

Council of Europe Publishing

French edition:

Droits de l'Homme – Handicap – Enfants
Vers des dispositions internationales pour les personnes
handicapées – Le cas particulier des enfants handicapés – Actes
de la conférence

ISBN-10: 92-871-5871-1
ISBN-13: 978-92-871-5871-0

Cover design: Graphic Design Workshop, Council of Europe
Layout: Desktop Publishing Unit, Council of Europe

Council of Europe Publishing
F-67075 Strasbourg Cedex
http://book.coe.int

ISBN-10: 92-871-5873-8
ISBN-13: 978-92-871-5873-4
© Council of Europe, December 2005
Printed in Germany

CONTENTS

INTRODUCTION

The Conference "Human Rights – Disability - Children: Towards international instruments for disability rights – the special case of disabled children" took place at the Council of Europe in Strasbourg, 8-9 November 2004.

The conference, organised by Directorate General III – Social Cohesion, under the aegis of the Norwegian Chairmanship of the Committee of Ministers, helped to promote the multidisciplinary and rights-based approach to disability issues, and the paradigm shift: "From the patient to the citizen".

The event was attended by more than 100 participants from 34 Council of Europe member and observer states, as well as 9 international and several national non-governmental organisations of people with disabilities, notably parents' associations. Participants were welcomed to the Council by the Secretary General, Mr Terry DAVIS, and the Conference was opened by Ms Kristin RAVNANGER, Secretary of State of Labour and Social Affairs of Norway, and closed by Mr Hans Olav SYVERSEN, Secretary of State for Family and Children Affairs of Norway. Conclusions were presented by Mr Alexander VLADYCHENKO, Director General ad interim of Social Cohesion (DG III).

The main topics discussed at the conference were:

- How do Council of Europe instruments protect and promote the human rights of people with disabilities?
- how can the forthcoming Council of Europe Disability Action Plan complement the draft United Nations Disability Convention and how can it help to implement the rights of disabled children and their families?

– how can we avoid putting disabled children into institutions and how can we encourage and enable parents with disabled children to take care of them at home?

The event clearly showed that disability is a pan-European issue, and that related activities should be carried out by all Council of Europe member and observer states. It also showed that too many people with disabilities still live in institutions and that community-based local service provision must be stepped up. This might be achieved in stages by firstly improving the quality of life in institutions, downsizing wherever possible, decentralising administration and funding and making the accommodation as homely as possible. Building up options for mainstreaming and community-based support services will require trained staff, attention to detailed assessment and person-centred planning, backed up by solid support to families and carers.

In order to uphold the rights of children, women and men with disabilities, member states need to:
– define and prioritise the rights of disabled children and adults both in generic and specialist instruments;
– implement those instruments;
– actively support anti-discrimination measures;
– assure access to equitable health care and social support services;
– support persons with disabilities and their families in exercising these rights.

Concrete follow-up to the conference will be provided by a multidisciplinary ad hoc group of experts to be set up in Directorate General III – Social Cohesion to elaborate recommendations and guidelines on deinstitutionalisation of children with disabilities in order to allow them to live with their family and in their community. The group will also elaborate a strategy to assist member states with the implementation of those recommendations and guidelines.

GENERAL REPORT

Human Rights – Disability – Children:
Towards international instruments for disability rights: the special case of disabled children

Prof. Hilary BROWN, Professor of Social Care,
Canterbury Christ Church University College,
United Kingdom

The Secretary General of the Council of Europe, Mr Terry Davis, opened the conference by reminding participants that progress in our countries must be judged, not only by economic measures but also by the ability of states to include and protect all citizens. He estimated that there were 80 million people with disabilities in Council of Europe member states and that consequently, disability policy issues concerned all of them. Further work to break down social stereotypes and challenge prejudice was urged. But he reminded the conference that many children, women and men with disabilities continue to experience isolation, stigma, social exclusion and institutionalisation and reiterated the need for attitude change as well as policy and service development across all member states.

The Secretary of State of the Norwegian Ministry of Labour and Social Affairs, Ms Kristin Ravnanger, chaired the conference and spoke of the shared commitment to promote the dignity and human rights of all citizens and to take action against discrimination on grounds of disability as core values across all member states. She expressed the priority attached to this agenda under Norway's Chairmanship of the Council of Europe and reaffirmed the commitment spelt out at the 2003 Ministerial Conference in Malaga to work towards full human rights for disabled women and men, and also to pay special attention to the needs of disabled children and their families.

Exercising rights on behalf of children is especially important. Their ability to participate on an equal basis in adult life will depend on early intervention and support for their families and on access to mainstream childcare and education so that they experience inclusion from the beginning. Segregated services further disadvantage children and handicap them unnecessarily.

All Council of Europe members, observer states and NGOs had signed up to this commitment in Malaga and had made formal decisions to take disabled people and their families more into account, through improved access, better service provision and most of all through inclusion at all levels of our economic, political, social, and cultural life.

Building on this consensus the conference was convened to:

– disseminate and strengthen the impact of current legal and political instruments;

– herald new initiatives including the proposed UN Comprehensive and Integral International Convention on the Protection and Promotion of the Rights and Dignity of Persons with Disabilities and the Council of Europe Disability Action Plan;

– work towards a "roadmap" to set out important steps in turning this political will into action.

The policy context

The importance of this anti-discrimination and pro-human rights agenda for people with disabilities is not only being embraced by European states within the Council of Europe but also globally within by the United Nations. Existing protection is enshrined in generic instruments, such as the UN Declaration of Human Rights, the European Convention on Human Rights, the European Social Charter and the UN Convention on the Rights of the Child. Furthermore, work is

8

underway on two important instruments which are specific to disabled people, such as the UN draft convention on disability and the Council of Europe Disability Action Plan. The UN document will be a legally binding instrument, the Council of Europe Disability Action Plan a morally binding political commitment to action.

The Council of Europe Disability Action Plan

The Council of Europe Disability Action Plan builds on Recommendation R (92) 6 on a Coherent Policy for People with Disabilities and on the deliberations of the 2003 Malaga Ministerial Conference. It will act as the means for sustaining their momentum and implementing the proposed UN convention across Europe. It will emphasise the need for de-institutionalisation and for a parallel growth in support to parents and carers, and these themes were explored in parallel workshops.

Mr Hans Sluiter (the Netherlands), Chairman of the Disability Action Plan Drafting Group, shared progress and spoke of the important shift from a primarily medical model to one rooted in commitment to universal human rights. He described it as a political, as opposed to a legal, instrument in that it sets out a detailed implementation plan and he urged delegates to input material and ideas through their national delegates. Each action line is elaborated through an introduction, clearly stated objectives, a programme of specific actions for member states and for the Council of Europe to undertake and a reference to cross-cutting issues and the implications for those in need of a high level of support, for children and for women with disabilities.

The plan as formulated should facilitate clear reporting and monitoring and it was pointed out in the discussion that an independent monitoring system to evaluate implementation would strengthen the plan's influence. In the closing plenary session Mr Reinertsen of the Permanent Representation of Norway to the Council of Europe echoed the commitment to follow-up, with particular view to the forthcoming 3rd Council of Europe Summit of Heads of State and Government in Warsaw in May 2005.

Other disability-related work within the Council of Europe

Representatives from the European Court of Human Rights and the Directorate General of Human Rights spoke of the Council of Europe's long tradition of championing the rights of disabled people through the Convention on Human Rights, the Social Charter and the work of the Committee for the Prevention of Torture, Inhuman and Degrading Treatment, which has been especially active in relation to people with mental health problems and those detained in psychiatric services. The Working Party on Bioethics has also played a part in protecting disabled people from intrusive and unethical research and has been working on consent issues where disabled people are being held against their will. Meanwhile Recommendation R(99)4 on principles concerning the legal protection of incapable adults has set international standards on legislation in relation to people who lack capacity to make their own decisions and on safeguards for those who are unable to act in, or protect, their own interests.

The Council of Europe Development Bank (CEB) has played an active role in funding and underwriting the restructuring of institutional service provision and the building up of more inclusive, community-based services. But it is widely acknowledged that there is a lot more to be done and that many disabled children are still deprived of a real childhood by being placed in institutions, while women and men with disabilities continue to face pervasive discrimination in employment, housing and income, which cuts across their autonomy and inclusion.

The Commissioner for Human Rights visits member states to monitor whether case law is being put into practice and to report on sensitive issues. The Commissioner always inspects psychiatric and children's services recognising the potential for human rights violations in these settings and it consults widely with NGOs in advance of its visits. Mr Manuel

Lezertua, representing the Commissioner, spoke of concerns including:

- lack of clarity leading to an "elastic" definition of disability across member states, with confusion especially around whether the term is being used to include people with HIV related illnesses, or those with mental health problems;

- continuation of the practice of placing people with physical or sensory impairments in psychiatric institutions as well as routine failure to discriminate between those with intellectual and psychiatric disabilities;

- the cumulative impact of social exclusion for disabled children and adults from minority ethnic groups especially Roma and other travelling peoples and refugees who are amongst the most discriminated against in Europe;

- the failure of states to work actively to promote changed attitudes and to apply sanctions for continued discrimination or harassment against disabled people;

- challenges in protecting human rights in specialist institutions typified by Amnesty International's recent campaign against the use of cage beds and the use of brutal and unauthorised "control and restraint" techniques with disturbed or disturbing patients: these institutions continue to operate without enough, let alone enough trained, staff to guarantee even minimal standards of care; and while living conditions have improved generally across member states disabled children and adults are still dying for want of adequate heating, nourishment and activities and are still living in places which bear more resemblance to prisons than to homes;

- the Court has adjudicated in recent cases of people being placed against their will but without formal hearings or safeguards and without measures to respect their choices or decisions in everyday matters.

It was made clear that the placing of children into institutions should be seen as a last resort. States should be using the current instruments to:

11

- prioritise efforts to abolish all forms of discrimination;

- facilitate support, training and financial help to families with the specific aim of preventing institutional placement especially of children;

- improve living conditions in institutions because even small improvements can make the difference between life and death to many people;

- never lose sight of the overarching goal of participation and full human rights for disabled persons.

The role of the European Court of Human Rights

Mr Loukis Loucaides, Judge in respect of Cyprus at the European Court of Human Rights, spoke of the Court's intervention in enforcing the Convention on Human Rights on behalf of disabled people, reminding the conference that disabled children and adults are included within these instruments and that the rights set out in these articles belong to everyone. The Court is incrementally producing case law and setting progressive obligations on member states to improve the situation of disabled women, men and children.

The 2003 Malaga Ministerial Conference on Disability had spelt out the need for states to combat indirect as well as direct discrimination and especially to address those situations in which failure to treat a disabled child or adult differently would lead to inequitable treatment or disadvantage, for example in relation to health or education. States have to recognise diversity and act in ways that assure "real and effective equality". A similar principle has been upheld in relation to assistance for children in mainstream education right up to tertiary level studies. Children with autism, for example, cannot be maintained in mainstream school placements without attention being paid to assistance and the training of staff to support them; case law in this area is working to clarify what is expected and to mandate the state's efforts to make mainstreaming work before justifying placement in special institutions or segregated services. These cases are beginning to define the extent to which member states should take

12

proactive steps to achieve integration even where this necessitates proactive steps to overcome the state of learned helplessness induced in those detained in institutions. Consideration should be given to according sign language the status of an official language and recognising Braille as an official literacy system.

Recent case law has also made clear that there can be no exceptions to Article 3 which prohibits torture as upheld in a recent judgment on the detention of a severely disabled person in a prison without proper facilities, which was deemed to constitute a violation, as was the failure to provide proper psychiatric care to a prisoner with mental health problems who later committed suicide. Interrogation and deportation might also constitute a violation as was the case in a recent hearing involving an Algerian citizen who was deaf but who had lived all his life in France who successfully argued that he would be isolated if he was returned.

Article 5 has also been reiterated in recent hearings making clear that depriving anyone of their liberty must be done through formal and transparent mechanisms and accompanied by formal safeguards, including:

– that the person is suffering from an objective medical condition;
– that the nature of their disability is such that they constitute a risk to themselves or others;
– that they are detained only as long as this condition persists and that their condition is regularly reviewed;
– and that there are accessible mechanisms to challenge the decision.

Children's rights to a fair trial have been upheld for example in a recent case brought against the United Kingdom in which an 11-year-old child had been tried in an adult criminal court despite his immaturity and limited intellectual ability.

Article 8 is being upheld in ways that make clear that the right to family privacy does not trump the right to physical and psychological integrity of children or women, within the family. In

13

discussion this point was reiterated and it was emphasised that children sometimes need protection from, not only with, their families. Disabled children should not be disadvantaged within the child protection systems of our countries and when there are conflicts of interest it should be quite clear that the interests of the child take primacy over the wishes or decisions of their parents or carers.

States also have to act assertively on behalf of disabled people as victims of crime to assure their equitable access to justice, as was reiterated in a recent case against the Netherlands in which a 16-year-old mentally disabled girl who was raped, had subsequently been denied justice because she was required to be the one to trigger the criminal justice system. In debate delegates pointed out that access to civil remedies was also often blocked by lack of money or legal aid as disabled people by and large, do not have sufficient income to risk taking legal action in pursuance of their rights, or to challenge their status, living conditions or treatment. Bulgarian and Turkish delegates were particularly concerned with this issue and with a shortage of suitably qualified and committed lawyers. Recourse to law may also be blocked in situations where there is a fear of recriminations, or a fear that the person will be removed from whatever services that exist, even where these are inadequate.

Protocol 2 of Article 1 has been used to explore rights to mainstream education and finds in favour of this right although with caveats if the mainstream system has reached its limits, whether financial or professional. States have an obligation to pursue positive measures to facilitate integration, including through enforcing access or providing state of the art prosthetic devices or technical aids, but they are allowed to take economic considerations into account. This dilemma is particularly reflected in eastern European countries that experience difficulty in making headway for disabled children and adults against the backdrop of extreme poverty that engulfs all citizens.

Mr Régis Brillat, Directorate General of Human Rights, spoke about the European Social Charter, a treaty signed in 1961 and revised in 1996, through which states guarantee to extend social and economic rights to all citizens: it had been ratified by 35 out of 46 countries and guaranteed rights in relation to housing, health, education, legal and social protection and migration. States are obligated to uphold these rights and return formal reports through which their progress is monitored and their concordance adjudicated. There is also a procedure whereby independent bodies such as NGOs or trade unions could lodge a collective complaint to trigger an investigation on behalf of a group of disabled people, although some states have not ratified this clause. Article 17 translated the provisions set out in the UN Convention on the Rights of the Child into European law. Use of the Social Charter is evolving and is still breaking new ground.

In parallel to this work the Council of Europe continues to undertake work by committees of experts such as the one currently meeting to address the needs of people with autism, who present a special challenge as the nature of their impairment strikes at the heart of their understanding of culture and relationships, leading them to feel like aliens in their own families and communities and exacerbating the sense of isolation which can affect many people with disabilities.

Rights in action

Two parallel workshops reflected twin strategies of deinstitutionalisation while at the same time building up the capacity of communities to support families and children.

Deinstitutionalisation

The first workshop, chaired by Mr Christian Kielland, Senior Adviser at the Ministry of Labour and Social Affairs, Norway, explored different strategies for deinstitutionalisation. Speakers were Prof. Jan Tøssebro (Norway) who spoke of the challenges of deinstitutionalisation, Ms Diana Hoover, Director of the Mental Disability Advocacy Centre (MDAC), Budapest, which acts as a Human Rights advocacy agency in eastern European countries particularly in relation to psychiatric services and Ms Bardhylka Kospiri of the Albanian Disability Rights Foundation.

Norway's experience of deinstitutionalisation has been long-standing. The movement for deinstitutionalisation rested on a shift of policy which was more philosophical than scientific in its underpinning, - there was no indication that new services would necessarily be cheaper or more "effective" but they represented a response to powerful critiques and naming of institutional practices, such as segregation and labelling, and to scandals about the actual living conditions of many people, which had exposed the inhumanity of these regimes. Basing his comments on a longitudinal study of families, Prof. Tøssebro acknowledged that some of these difficulties have been replaced by other forms of exclusion and alienation, brought about by loneliness, but reaffirmed the consensus around mainstreaming and the will to solve problems in this new arena.

Prof. Tøssebro 's paper suggested that it was now possible to acknowledge and explore problems in community facilities without always harking back to the past or giving up on the commitment to mainstreaming in education or inclusion in all aspects of living. In common with other countries, institutional placements peaked in Norway between 1945 and 1970 and he reported research demonstrating the international trend towards reduction of congregate services over the last two decades of the last century. This is paralleled by figures for placements in special boarding schools. Research has shown that mainstreaming in education has led to disabled people learning more and having better self-esteem. Although children were being accorded priority in those countries where institutional provision is most entrenched, deinstitutionalisation also represents a priority for adults, and it was said in discussion that disabled adults tend to face even more community hostility than children in countries where there is no history of integration.

16

Ms Hoover spoke of an increasing number of children being placed in institutions as economies and health care systems in eastern European countries experienced upheaval. Poverty drove parents to leave their children in institutions where there was no rehabilitation or route out and where as children and later as adults they would routinely face conditions that led to higher rates of mortality, malnutrition, hypothermia, abuse and overuse of medication. These situations represent an urgent as well as a chronic danger.

Ms Kospiri acknowledged the huge difficulties experienced by eastern European countries struggling with worsening economic conditions as market "reforms" were introduced into their countries: this makes a troubling backdrop to any major restructuring of welfare provision. Most people live below the poverty level and disabled people and their families tend to fall further into, or be more hopelessly trapped in, chronic poverty with its concomitant low self-esteem and restricted employment opportunities. It is hardly surprising that human rights violations are more rife in these conditions and more difficult to undo or redress.

Supporting children and families

The second parallel workshop was chaired by Mr Helmut Heinen of the Office for People with disabilities from the German-speaking community in Belgium, and explored detailed approaches to assessment, therapeutic intervention and individualised supports. Speakers were Ms Marie-Cecile Vadeau-Ducher (France), who linked the work to initiatives of the European Committee for Social Cohesion (CDCS). Ms Aase Frostad Fasting (Norway) spoke of a specific model for assessment and Mr Berger Hareide (Norway) described a comprehensive programme of social and emotional support for parents. Ms Marchita Mangiafico spoke of the realities for her as a single parent in Malta caring for a disabled son as he approached adulthood.

Deinstitutionalisation cannot work in isolation, families and carers need both practical, emotional and financial supports

17

to allow them to provide a decent quality of life for their children but also to do so in ways which do not isolate them or create unacceptable stress on their own relationship or on other children in the family. Many parents wished or needed to remain in the workforce. States embarking on this restructuring need either to provide services, or to provide economic rewards in lieu of a proper wage in acknowledgment of the work involved in the care of their disabled child so that deinstitutionalisation did not happen at the expense of parents. Extended networks and families are also important, grandparents may play a key role, and siblings also find themselves with a lifelong commitment. Parents often voice considerable anxiety about what will happen to their daughters and sons when they die or when they can no longer care for them: they deserve the assurance that comes from knowing there are appropriate services for their children which will maintain a high quality of life for their relative, anything less is an insupportable burden to older parents and a poor way of recognising their input to the welfare of our communities.

The issue of exceptional parental leave, and/or flexibility to attend appointments with children with special needs was also raised in the workshop and the plenary and unions were urged to play a part in negotiating on behalf of family members who wished to remain in, or could not afford to leave, the workforce. The reality as spoken by Ms Mangiafico showed how far many countries have to travel if individual parents are not to be left shouldering too great a responsibility on their own, in her case "shouldering" is literally what she has to do as she lives in a first floor flat and routinely carries her son upstairs with no change in sight even as he grows towards adulthood. Rights are abstract, but responsibilities seem very concrete and can be far too heavy if left to individuals to manage on their own.

Taking the issues forward

Mr Marc Maudinet, Director of the National Centre for Research on Disabilities and Social Exclusion, Paris, summarised important themes for the drafting group to take into

18

their deliberations. He spoke of people being in a "situation" of handicap not "suffering" from an illness and that they were primarily in need of social protection and action. Barriers to implementation of internationally agreed rights included unstable political climates and the need to strengthen partnerships with NGOs in a systematic way. He identified the importance of the following elements of a coherent programme:

- everyone having the possibility of living autonomously;
- broadening the range of accommodation available;
- allowing people to choose their own environments;
- getting rid of large units;
- developing common standards in relation to access;
- making urban spaces and products (IT and appliances) universally accessible.

Mr Stefan Trömel, European Disability Forum (EDF), presented the views of non-governmental disability organisations and stressed the need of involving people with disabilities, their families, their cares, and their representative organisations in any disability policy-making, and in any follow-up to be given to this Conference.

Mr Alexander Vladychenko, Director General ad interim of Social Cohesion summed up the main findings of the conference. He recalled that according to a WHO estimate some 10% of the population were affected by a disability. However, when families are taken into account, disability could be seen to affect as many as 30-40% of the population. He said that too many people with disabilities were still living in institutions and that resistance to local services must be broken down. This might be achieved in stages by firstly improving the quality of life in institutions, downsizing wherever possible, decentralising administration and funding and making the accommodation as homely as possible. Building up options for mainstreaming would require trained staff, attention to detailed assessment and person-centred planning, backed up by solid support to families and carers. The status quo cannot be allowed to continue as disabled people living within our communities currently experienced cumulative and debilitating disadvantages, with the result that as individuals and as a group:

- they are less well educated than others;
- they have less work;
- they experience the worst health outcomes;
- they live in the poorest accommodation and
- they have to endure lower incomes.

So the problem is multi-faceted: in order for states to uphold, as opposed to merely espouse, the rights of children, women and men with disabilities, they need to:

- define and prioritise the rights of disabled children and adults both in generic and specialist instruments;
- ratify the relevant articles;
- actively support anti-discrimination measures;
- proactively assure access to equitable health and welfare benefits;
- facilitate and fund access to justice;
- support individuals and their families in exercising these rights.

Concrete follow-up to the conference will be provided by a multidisciplinary ad hoc group of experts to be set up in Directorate General III – Social Cohesion to elaborate recommendations and guidelines on deinstitutionalisation of children with disabilities and provide assistance to member states as to their implementation.

Mr Alexander Vladychenko, Director General ad interim of Social Cohesion (DG III) finally thanked the Norwegian Presidency of the Committee of Ministers for the generous support, enabling DG III to organise this conference and its follow-up. By putting disability so high on the European political agenda, Norway provided the adequate follow-up to the European Year of Disabled People 2003 and the Council of Europe's Malaga Ministerial Conference on Disability. They were the first Presidency to have done so, but hopefully not the last.

The conference was officially closed by Mr Hans Olav Syverson, Secretary of State for Family and Children Affairs of Norway, who confirmed the Norwegian commitment to disability policies, in particular related to disabled children and their families. He stressed the need for immediate action both at national and international level, and assured the Council of Europe of continued Norwegian support in furthering the integration of disabled children and their families in their local communities, thus ending or avoiding their institutionalisation.

WELCOME ADDRESSES

Mr Terry DAVIS,
Secretary General of the Council of Europe

Secretary of State, Ladies and Gentlemen,

It is my great pleasure to be here today to open this very important conference, which will take a closer look at the situation of people with disabilities and in particular children with disabilities and their families, their special problems and needs, and how all of us – the Council of Europe, the governments of our member states, and civil society – can better protect and promote the rights of these children and help them to enjoy their lives in much the same way as everyone else.

Disability is clearly a pan-European issue, and dealing with it requires bold initiatives and concerted action across our continent. Much is already being done. It was both moving and inspiring to see the triumph of human spirit over disability during the Paralympic Games in Athens just two months ago. The images of athletes with various physical difficulties showing the true spirit of perseverance in achieving their goal and their dream must have surely convinced all of us that the full integration of people with disabilities and their participation in society is already a reality to a large extent.

However, there is still much more left to do. This is why I welcome the initiative to convene this conference and would like to express my gratitude to the Norwegian Chair of the Committee of Ministers for sponsoring it and for putting disability so high on the European political agenda. Your action in this field has helped to promote an approach to disability issues based on human rights, and to bring about the shift

"From the patient to the citizen". Your Chairmanship will end the day after tomorrow, so this really is your "Grand Finale".

Ladies and gentlemen, it is my firm belief that the strength of any society, the strength of a nation cannot be measured in terms of gross domestic product or per capita income alone. These are statistics. What we must focus on is how they affect people. The true strength of society and government lies in a fair distribution of welfare, in the ability to protect all of our citizens equally and fairly, paying special attention to the most vulnerable groups.

What we need today is a shift in both mentality and policy to make sure that people with disabilities are regarded not as patients but as citizens who enjoy the same rights as every-one else – appreciated as individuals, make decisions about their own lives, have access to education and employment, participate in the life of the community and enjoy culture, entertainment, tourism, leisure and sport.

How many of an estimated 80 million Europeans with disabil-ities feel treated this way and how many children with dis-abilities can say it?

In today's reality, children with disabilities and their families often face isolation, stigmatisation and social exclusion. Such families are often faced with insurmountable problems. The professional support they need is often not available. As a consequence, children are often institutionalised.

What can the Council of Europe do?

I hope that through this conference, you will help me to answer that question.

Ms Kristin RAVNANGER
Secretary of State for Labour and Social Affairs, Norway

Ladies and Gentlemen, Friends,

It is both a pleasure and an honour for me to address this conference on behalf of the Norwegian Chairmanship. I trust you will all have a useful and pleasant stay here, and I look forward to interesting presentations and discussions the next two days.

Norway is a founding member of the Council of Europe. We have always given high priority to the organisation and supported its work. In the Council of Europe we have a unique set of common values – human dignity, rule of law, mutual respect and reconciliation. The Council of Europe is a pan-European network, which safeguards the fundamental rights of 800 million citizens. During our chairmanship period we have striven to strengthen the role of the Council of Europe and adapt it to a changing European landscape. We have concentrated on the organisation's core values and areas of expertise, and we have tried to promote a constructive relationship with other European organisations.

Human rights have always been a core issue and primary concern of the Council of Europe. Human rights are rights for all human beings. But many of us have not been aware if the fact that human beings with disabilities are being discriminated against to such an extent that they cannot fully enjoy human rights on an equal basis with other persons.

The Conference of Ministers in Malaga last year changed this. The ministers reaffirmed their commitment to securing human rights and fundamental freedoms for everyone and that arrangements for the full and effective implementation of all human rights must be applicable without any discrimination or distinction on any ground, including disability.

Disability policies in the Council of Europe have until recently mostly been left to a group of especially interested member states. The Conference of Ministers in Malaga last year changed this, too. It invited all Council of Europe member and observer states and representatives from European non-governmental organisations to participate in the activities and work of the Council relating to disability policy. This was followed up by a formal decision of the Committee of Ministers. The Secretary General of the Council of Europe was asked to ensure that the disability dimension is better taken into consideration within the overall activities of the Council of Europe.

The Parliamentary Assembly's important recommendation "Towards full social inclusion of persons with disabilities", which was adopted even before the Malaga Conference, assures us that this approach has broad support throughout Europe. Our challenge now is to transform our intentions into legal and political documents that will be our road maps for an inclusive Europe.

This conference focuses on human rights for children with disabilities. We want to improve conditions for all persons with disabilities. But we feel that it is especially important to strive to provide equal opportunities for todays children with disabilities to participate in today's European society on an equal basis with other people.

European disability policy is shaped not only in a European context but also in a global context. The future international convention on the protection and promotion of the rights and dignity of persons with disabilities, which is being negotiated at the United Nations, will – I hope – be signed and ratified by all European states. We should, therefore, play an active role in these negotiations, as many European countries have, indeed, done so far. The Council of Europe Disability Action Plan, which is being drafted as a follow-up to the Malaga Ministerial Conference, should be seen as our plan for implementing the future convention.

At this conference we will first present and discuss the European human rights framework for disability policies. We then introduce what is a central theme in present day disability policy – deinstitutionalisation. As will be seen from the presentations, the centrality of this theme will be reflected both in the UN international convention and in the Council of Europe Disability Action Plan.

Deinstitutionalisation is also the theme also of the conference's workshop No. 1. Challenges of deinstitutionalisation will be presented, with reference to experience in both my own country and other countries. For persons with mental disabilities a life outside institutions is often considered to present more challenges than for other people with disabilities. We also want to discuss the problems of countries which have a stronger tradition for large institutions than other countries. We should, however, keep in mind that institutional thinking is alive in all European countries. Finally, we want to pay special attention to the parents of children with disabilities. What does a policy of deinstitutionalisation do to their lives?

Workshop No. 2 goes into more depth on the lives of disabled children and their families. The Council of Europe's revised strategy for social cohesion will be presented, with particular attention to its implications for the inclusion of disabled children in mainstream society. The future of children with disabilities is fundamentally influenced by the attitudes that we have towards disability. Is it the child's disability that is important to us? Or is it the child itself and all potentialities that the individual person has? If we want an inclusive society, we need to concentrate more on abilities than disabilities. This theme will be discussed in the light of practical experience and scientific research. And, again, we focus on disabled children living not in institutions but with their families. So we pay special attention to the challenges that these families are faced with. The theme will be presented both from the service providers' perspective and from the parents' perspective.

Tomorrow we will concentrate on consequences for the two important policy documents – the Council of Europe Disability Action Plan and the United Nations convention. Will they really help persons with disabilities? In what ways? What can we do to make them efficient instruments?

Since this is a Council of Europe conference, we pay particular attention to how the items to be discussed these two days should be reflected in our own Disability Action Plan. We hope that our discussions will be useful to the Drafting Group.

This is the last in a series of Norwegian chairmanship events. Our chairmanship ends on Wednesday. I therefore feel a certain pride in being allowed to chair this conference. Its theme fits in nicely with Norwegian priorities in the Council of Europe. Human rights are important to us. So are disability policies. We took the initiative, in co-operation with other countries, pursuant the recommendation of the Malaga Ministerial Conference that disability issues should be mainstreamed within the Council of Europe organisation. The recommendation concerns all our member states and all policy areas.

I would like to thank the Council of Europe Secretariat for following up the recommendation in a constructive spirit, and for the competent job they have done with this conference.

The idea behind this conference is that we should all learn something from it, to help us improve our own performance. We must continually ask ourselves how we can improve our own record on human rights for children – and adults - with disabilities. We must focus both on our individual national policies and on the Council of Europe's contribution. This is the challenge to you, ladies and gentlemen! Let us go to this task in a friendly spirit of co-operation!

Thank you for your attention.

HUMAN RIGHTS FRAMEWORK

The Council of Europe and the protection and promotion of the human rights of people with disabilities

Mr Manuel LEZERTUA,
Director of the Office of the Council of Europe
Human Rights Commissioner

The Council of Europe has a long standing tradition of protecting people with disabilities, and the European Convention on Human Rights and, subsequently, the European Social Charter, have proved to be effective means of upholding such people's rights. The organisation has also adopted other standard-setting instruments that afford people with disabilities enhanced protection at all stages in their lives. Alongside these legal instruments, the Council has structures designed to assist policy development in the social and public health fields.

Undeniable progress has been made in Europe over recent decades. The perception of disability has gradually shifted so that the emphasis is no longer on dependence and assistance but on autonomy and integration. A large number of the institutions in which people with disabilities were traditionally cut off from the rest of society have been closed or have undergone far-reaching reforms. In this connection, mention must be made of the key role played by the Council of Europe Development Bank, which helps states to develop and fund programmes for the construction and renovation of centres and homes.

Nonetheless, much remains to be done in order to bridge the gap between theory and practice. All too often, findings of the Commissioner for Human Rights have shown that people with disabilities are excluded from the mainstream community, treated as social outcasts and suffer discrimination and prejudice.

The Council of Europe is active in seeking solutions to these problems. To pinpoint some of the obstacles that people with disabilities come up against in asserting their fundamental rights, reference can be made to the legal instruments devised by the Council of Europe with a view to protecting their rights.

In addition to the European Convention on Human Rights and the European Social Charter, the Convention for the Prevention of Torture and Inhuman or Degrading Treatment or Punishment guarantees respect for the rights of persons deprived of their liberty, including people with disabilities placed in institutions. The Committee for the Prevention of Torture (CPT), established under the convention, conducts inspection visits of detention facilities in prisons and police stations, in particular, but also of psychiatric hospitals, institutions for children with disabilities and children's homes. It then prepares reports assessing the living conditions prevailing in the establishments visited, taking account of the legislation covering the categories of persons concerned.

As mentioned above, the Council of Europe also pursues activities in the field of disability policy, in particular through the Partial Agreement in the Social and Public Health Field. The purpose of this agreement is to protect public health and allow the rehabilitation and integration of people with disabilities. Its activities are pursued through committees of experts and working groups responsible for drawing up recommendations and guidelines in this sphere. The Committee on the Rehabilitation and Integration of People with disabilities, for instance, aims to guarantee such persons their independence and full enjoyment of their rights. This committee has laid down general policy principles in this area, which, in 1992, the

Committee of Ministers of the Council of Europe incorporated into its Recommendation No. R (92) 6 on a coherent policy for people with disabilities.

Convinced of the need for action, the Committee of Ministers and the Parliamentary Assembly are also instrumental in enhancing respect for disability rights.

The Committee of Ministers adopted Recommendation No.R (99) 4 on principles concerning the legal protection of incapable adults and Recommendation Rec(2004)10 concerning the protection of the human rights and dignity of persons with mental disorders. The latter lays down a number of general provisions, including the principles of non-discrimination, full enjoyment of civil and political rights by people with disabilities, information on patients' rights and protection of vulnerable persons with mental disorders. However, a large part of the text is devoted to the criteria, principles and procedures to be complied with in the event of involuntary placement or treatment and the rights of persons subject to such measures.

The Parliamentary Assembly of the Council of Europe for its part adopted two recommendations of direct relevance to people with disabilities in 2003. Recommendation 1592, entitled "Towards full social inclusion of persons with disabilities", focuses on the efforts that remain to be made at state level, particularly in terms of social inclusion and access to the labour market. It also sets out the measures to be taken by the Council of Europe itself to facilitate full integration of people with disabilities. Recommendation 1601, entitled "Improving the lot of abandoned children in institutions", calls for the earliest possible diagnosis of disability in children and for full safeguards surrounding decisions to place children in institutions, entailing regular review and provision for appeal procedures.

The activities of the Commissioner for Human Rights related to the protection of people with disabilities are an extension of the Council of Europe's work in this field. The Commissioner's mandate is to contribute to the promotion of the effective observance and full enjoyment of human rights in the member states, identify possible shortcomings in their law and practice and assist them, with their agreement, in their efforts to remedy such shortcomings. Lastly, he co-operates with human rights structures in the member states and, where such structures do not exist, encourages their establishment.

Under the terms of this mandate the Commissioner conducts fact-finding visits in Council of Europe member states. These visits enable him to form a direct, independent opinion on the human rights situation in the member state concerned and to issue relevant recommendations. Visits are arranged so as to include meetings with heads of state and ministers - particularly those responsible for justice, home affairs, health and foreign affairs - and with representatives of parliament, the judiciary, national human rights protection bodies, where these exist, and human rights NGOs.

During his visits the Commissioner also inspects premises where respect for fundamental rights is a particularly sensitive issue, such as prisons, refugee camps and psychiatric hospitals. Following the visit the Commissioner draws up a report for the Committee of Ministers and the Parliamentary Assembly, which is published on the Internet and which sets out his opinion on the human rights situation in the country concerned.

During each visit the Commissioner attaches special importance to the observance of disability rights and seeks to verify that people with disabilities are guaranteed full enjoyment of their rights both in law and in practice. To that end, he is in regular contact with NGOs dealing with such matters. The Commissioner is conscious of the work done in this field by both local and international NGOs, which, day in, day out, fulfil a vital role in protecting and upholding the rights of people with disabilities and providing them and their families with advice and support. During his visits the Commissioner has meetings with government agencies responsible for welfare matters in order to discuss any problems with them. Lastly, if he deems necessary he may visit an institution or specialist centre in order to conduct direct interviews with staff or residents.

The Commissioner also holds seminars on specific themes linked to the protection of human rights. Having found that the situation of people with disabilities is not always accorded sufficient importance, the Commissioner has taken a number of initiatives in this sphere. To mark the European Year of People with Disabilities 2003, he co-organised a seminar with WHO on the promotion and protection of the human rights of persons with mental disabilities, which was held in Copenhagen in February 2003. The aim was to propose solutions to the many problems encountered by disabled people in exercising their fundamental rights. The seminar's conclusions draw attention to the need for consultation when taking decisions affecting these persons, the need for appropriate treatment and services and, lastly, the need to involve all the players concerned: the state, local authorities, NGOs, families and the persons themselves. The Commissioner also spoke on these issues at the European Congress on People with Disabilities, held in Madrid in March 2002, and the Second European Conference of Ministers responsible for Integration Policies for People with Disabilities, held in Malaga in May 2003.

On the basis of these various events and his field observations, the Commissioner has identified a number of problems linked to respect for the rights of people with disabilities that are frequent throughout Europe. These problems are described in brief below.

Defining disability

The Commissioner has noted some very broad acceptations of the term disability, even going so far as to regard anyone in need of special care as disabled. In some countries, for instance, people infected with HIV or suffering from AIDS qualify as disabled. At a more general level, during visits to institutions for people with mental problems the Commissioner has often noted that people with physical disabilities have been placed there for lack of room in more suitable facilities. This often means that the people concerned do not receive appropriate care.

33

Non-discrimination

People with disabilities encounter obstacles in asserting their rights. Human rights must be guaranteed for all, not by treating everyone on an equal footing but by paying particular heed to the needs of the most vulnerable members of society. At the same time, even greater attention must be paid to people with disabilities who also suffer discrimination on other grounds: women, members of minority communities, immigrants or children. The Commissioner considers that these population groups, for whom the risk of exclusion is multiplied, should be the first to enjoy enhanced protection. To combat discrimination, what is needed is a commitment by society as a whole, a change in people's attitudes. Governments have a fundamental role to play here by seeking to raise awareness of these issues, setting a good example through improved integration of people with disabilities within their own structures and taking a stern attitude towards penalising discrimination so as to enforce respect for difference and for human dignity.

Respect for human rights in specialist institutions

As pointed out in the conclusions of the seminar held in Copenhagen, placement in a specialist institution must be a last resort. Accordingly states have a duty to afford people with disabilities the widest possible range of services within the community. Disability is not a disease but a permanent condition, and appropriate solutions must be found so that people affected can live as normal a life as possible. Social inclusion first and foremost entails making it possible for the person concerned to live within the community. However, placement in a specialist institution is sometimes unavoidable as the ultimate solution.

Placement in institutions

Placement should be voluntary and be arranged only with the informed consent of the person concerned. However, compulsory placement may be envisaged in exceptional circumstances. This minimum guarantee of consent must necessarily go hand in hand with the possibility for the person to challenge the placement decision in the courts, as for any other decision depriving an individual of his or her liberty. Regular review of the decision by a judicial authority must also be provided for. The Commissioner regards this supervisory mechanism as absolutely essential to prevent abuse of the placement process leading to violations of personal freedom.

Admitting a child to an institution must also be envisaged only as a last resort. It must be borne in mind that a child's place is with his or her family or people close to him or her, not in an institution. Placement must be considered only when it is in the child's best interests, as it can have very serious implications for his or her personal development. To avoid such situations arising, family members and friends must be offered alternative solutions and appropriate support. The Commissioner considers that the will to reduce institutionalisation must go hand in hand with the adoption of information and support measures targeting the families concerned.

Ill-treatment

Care must be taken to prevent ill-treatment of residents within institutions, who often have scant means of defending themselves. During inspection visits the Commissioner has frequently come across extremely competent members of staff, who show great respect for those in their care, but has also observed instances of real abuse, particularly in more isolated institutions. More often than not, ill-treatment takes the form of a heavy-handed reaction to agitated behaviour by a resident. Lack of adequate training of supervisory staff frequently worsens such situations. Instances of resident-on-resident abuse can also be observed where institutions are understaffed.

Living conditions

Living conditions in facilities for people with disabilities can generally be regarded as satisfactory. However, during visits to certain institutions in remote locations, the Commissioner has had occasion to note cases of inadequate care or pure neglect, understaffing, poorly trained staff, lack of food and heating and inappropriate accommodation.

Unfortunately, some of the premises visited were more reminiscent of a prison than a place designed to foster personal well-being and development. It is to be regretted that the living conditions prevailing in some institutions are tantamount to inhuman and degrading treatment and that deaths still occur in such facilities in Europe for lack of food and heating. States have a responsibility towards these people and are duty-bound to protect them and ensure that they receive decent treatment.

Preserving autonomy and legal capacity

It is essential that disability policies should address the issues of self-determination, independence and individual autonomy and that these should be a primary concern in all activities. The chief consideration when taking protection measures must be to uphold the dignity of the person concerned. Disability must never be synonymous with incapacity to take decisions for oneself or with deprivation of the right to defend one's interests. The Commissioner is still all too often informed of cases where people with disabilities have been denied access to a lawyer or to impartial, well-informed advice or where their complaints have been given no hearing. The Commissioner also deems it important that people with disabilities should have full access to justice, like any other individual.

Families' role

Attention must be drawn to the invaluable, irreplaceable role played by the families and friends of people with disabilities. In the case of children with disabilities, in particular, the Commissioner has on many occasions received testimonies showing how important support and assistance for parents and other family members can be to a child's well-being and individual development. He has also noted that too little recognition is given to family members and that the need to provide them with appropriate assistance is all too often disregarded.

The current efforts to make children with disabilities more autonomous and facilitate their integration, rather than rapidly placing them in an institution, confer a key role on their families. It must be ensured that such families are given greater moral and financial support and have improved access to home help and other services. Making such assistance available to families is the most effective means of avoiding institutionalisation.

In conclusion, I wish to underline the objectives which the Commissioner for Human Rights has set regarding respect for the fundamental rights of people with disabilities. These are pursuit of the efforts to protect such people against discrimination on account of their disability, but also on other grounds such as age, ethnic origin or gender, and implementation of genuine, consistent disability policies, taking account not just of these persons' needs but also of their legitimate expectations. Lastly, living conditions in institutions must be improved: this is an area where investing a little money can change a great deal for residents.

The above general objectives also apply to children with disabilities, but in their case other objectives can be added, such as support for families through financial measures, appropriate assistance schemes and training. It is where disability is taken into account at the youngest possible age that its impact on a child's development can be limited.

The role of the European Court of Human Rights in the protection of the rights and dignity of people with disabilities

Mr Loukis LOUCAIDES,
Judge in respect of Cyprus
at the European Court of Human Rights

Introduction

The European Convention on Human Rights guarantees certain human rights for the benefit of individuals in general within the jurisdiction of the contracting parties. The Convention does not deal with any specific rights for the protection of persons with disabilities nor does it address in any way problems concerning such persons.

Of course the rights set out in the Convention belong to every individual including persons with one or another kind of disability. Article 14 of the Convention provides that the enjoyment of the rights safeguarded in the Convention shall be secured without discrimination on any ground such as sex, race, colour... national or social origin..., birth or other status. This excludes discrimination at the expense of disabled persons in the enjoyment of any of the rights under the Convention. However, what is of particular interest of the purposes of our topic are the following two questions:

a) Whether the difficulties, practical problems or special situation of disabled persons are taken into account so as to ensure effective enjoyment of the rights in question and,

b) Whether the state Parties to the Convention have an obligation to take positive measures to assist disabled persons to overcome their problems as much as possible.

The answer to the first question is positive. The Convention has always been considered to be an instrument capable of adapting itself to new developments and, for this reason, it was described in the case-law as a "living instrument"[1]. The adaptation and extension of the Convention has been effected through the interpretation of its provisions by the European Commission and the Court of Human Rights in the light of the changing conditions of life and the prevailing conceptions and values in democratic societies. While the Convention does not expressly refer to disability (with the single exception of Article 5(1)e infra.), applications brought by disabled persons have, over the years, given the Court and the Commission the opportunity to elaborate significant principles of case law in this area, as the following survey shows.

---

1. eg *Tyrer v. United Kingdom*, Series A no. 26 para 31.

Article 3 – Prohibition of torture

This provision enshrines one of the fundamental values of democratic society, admitting of no exceptions. In its first judgment under this provision,[1] the Court held that in assessing the severity of the punishment or treatment endured by a person, regard should be had to the victim's personal characteristics, such as their age, sex and state of health. Applying this case law in a recent judgment,[2] the Court found that the detention of a severely disabled woman for three nights and four days in a prison that lacked adequate facilities constituted degrading treatment and thus a violation of Article 3.

It is established case law under Article 3 that states are under an obligation to protect the physical and mental health of prisoners and detainees.[3] The Court has laid emphasis on the increased vulnerability in such situations of persons suffering mental illness, who may not be capable of complaining about their treatment. In a recent case the Court found that the failure to ensure adequate psychiatric care for a mentally disturbed prisoner who eventually committed suicide in his cell violated Article 3, since it amounted to inhuman and degrading treatment.[4]

The very fact of being disabled as such makes the person concerned particularly vulnerable to inhuman or degrading treatment. Certain prison conditions, interrogation techniques, deportation measures and similar restrictions of human rights, which are in general permissible under domestic or international human rights law, may amount to inhuman or degrading treatment if applied to a disabled person.[5] The Commission of Human Rights decided that the expulsion of

1. *Ireland v. United Kingdom*, Judgment of 18 January 1978, Series A No. 25.
2. *Price v. United Kingdom*, No. 33394/96, ECHR 2001-VII.
3. *Herzcegfalvy v. Austria*, Judgment of 24 September 1992, Series A No. 296-A.
4. *Keenan v. United Kingdom*, No. 27229/95, ECHR 2001-III.
5. Novak and Suntinger, The right of disabled persons not to be subjected to torture inhuman or degrading treatment or punishment in Human rights and disabled persons Essays and Relevant Human Rights Instruments p.117 and p.118

an Algerian citizen who had lived since his childhood in France constituted a violation of his right to personal integrity and respect for his family file under Articles 3 and 8 of the European Convention on Human Rights (ECHR). Taking into account the fact that the victim was deaf, the Commission found that his deportation to Algeria would inevitably lead to total sensory isolation constituting inhuman and degrading treatment.

So far as mentally disabled persons are concerned the European Court of Human Rights stressed in the case of Herczegfalvy v. Austria that "the position of inferiority and powerlessness which is typical of patients in psychiatric hospitals calls for increased vigilance in reviewing that the Convention has been complied with".

Article 5 – Right to liberty and security

The Court has consistently stressed the central importance of Article 5 in the scheme of Convention rights. Persons may be deprived of their liberty only if their situation is one of those set forth in the first paragraph. One of these concerns persons of unsound mind (sub-paragraph e). In the course of many judgments, the Court has clarified the substantive and procedural guarantees that must be observed before a person may be detained on the ground of mental disorder:[1] there must be objective medical evidence of the person's condition; the nature of their condition must be such as to necessitate compulsory confinement, i.e. where there is a danger of self-harm or harm to others; the confinement may only continue for as long as this condition persists. Furthermore, the place and conditions of detention must relate to the person's disorder.[2] Anyone detained on this basis is entitled to be informed of the reason in accordance with Article 5 § 2.[3] They must also have the opportunity to challenge the lawfulness of their detention

---

1. *Winterwerp v. Netherlands*, Judgment of 24 October 1979, Series A No 33.
2. *Ashingdane v. United Kingdom*, Judgment of 28 May 1985, Series A No. 93.
3. *Van der Leer v. Netherlands*, Judgment of 21 February 1990, Series A No. 170.

"speedily" and at regular intervals in accordance with Article 5 §4.

The Court has emphasised that a person detained on the ground of mental disorder should receive legal assistance for this purpose, in view of the importance of what is at stake – their liberty – and their diminished mental capacity.[1]

Article 6 – Right to a fair trial

In ensuring that the right of a fair trial is enjoyed effectively by disabled persons, it is submitted that all the necessary facilities for an effective conduct of proceedings on behalf of them and an effective exercise of the right of defence in a criminal case against them should be provided by the state. For instance, if the disabled person concerned is deaf or blind he/she should be given the necessary assistance to follow the judicial proceedings. In a recent judgement of the Court in the case of S.C. v. the United Kingdom the 4th Section found that Article 6 § 1 of the Convention has been violated because the Court was not convinced that in the circumstances of the case the 11-year-old applicant charged with attempted robbery was capable of participating effectively in his trial taking into account his young age and limited intellectual capacity. According to the same judgment the applicant should have been tried by "a specialist tribunal which is able to give full consideration to and make proper allowance for the handicaps under which he labours, and adapt its procedure accordingly".[2]

Article 8 – Right to respect for private and family life

The notion of private life, within the meaning of Article 8 has been given a broad reading. Indeed the Court has stated that the term is not susceptible to exhaustive definition.[3] The right to respect for private life has been clearly identified with the right to the free development of personality. The case law has

---

1. *Megyeri v. Germany*, Judgment of 12 May 1992, Series A No. 237-B.
2. 60958/00, judgment 15/06/2004.
3. *Ben Said v. United Kingdom*, No. 44599/98, ECHR 2001-I.

also established that the concept embraces physical and psychological integrity. A particularly important precedent in this field is the case of X. and Y v. Netherlands.[1] The applicants complained that a lacuna in Dutch law made it impossible to prosecute a man who had raped a mentally disabled girl aged 16 (the second applicant), since a criminal complaint had to be lodged by the victim herself, with no exception made for persons lacking legal capacity. The Court ruled that Article 8 required effective deterrence of such wrongdoing, which could only be ensured through the criminal law. Mere civil remedies were insufficient.

The landmark case of Pretty v. United Kingdom[2] raised fundamental questions about private life, illness, quality of life and personal autonomy. Ms. Pretty was at an advanced stage of a degenerative disease that left her severely physically incapacitated. She argued on the basis of several provisions of the Convention, including Article 8, that she had a "right to die" and that, accordingly, her husband should be permitted to assist her in ending her life. The Court affirmed that "[t]he very essence of the Convention is respect for human dignity and human freedom. Without in any way negating the principle of sanctity of life protected under the Convention, the Court considers that it is under Article 8 that notions of the quality of life take on significance." Although it went on to rule that the ban on assisted suicide was justified, this statement of principle is clearly relevant to the question of disability.

Article 1 of Protocol No. 1 – Protection of property

The case law regarding property and pecuniary rights has evolved over the years to the point where both contributory[3] and non-contributory[4] benefits are now considered to come within the scope of this provision. Although states enjoy a considerable margin of appreciation regarding the level of

---

1. Judgment of 26 March 1985, Series A No. 91.
2. No. 2346/02, ECHR 2002-III.
3. *Willis v. United Kingdom*, No. 36042/97, ECHR 2002-IV.
4. *Koua Poirrez v. France.*

payment, the right to social security or social welfare now enjoys the protection of the Convention and so cannot be arbitrarily taken away. Furthermore, since the right to receive such benefits clearly constitutes a civil right within the meaning of Article 6 § 1, legal proceedings concerning them must provide all the guarantees of fairness set forth in that provision: access to an independent and impartial court of law,[1] equality of arms, right to an oral hearing,[2] legal aid if necessary etc.

Article 2 of Protocol No. 1 – Right to education

The Commission considered an application brought by the parents of a child with mental and physical disabilities.[3] They argued that their son was entitled to be educated in the ordinary school system rather than being referred to specialised institutes and that the authorities should recognise and respect their firm conviction on this point. The Commission noted that under the relevant domestic legislation, children with special needs were educated in ordinary schools as far as possible. However, it observed that in some cases, more specialised education would be necessary. Accordingly, while the authorities had to place weight on the applicants' convictions, they were not under a duty to comply with their wishes regarding the education of their son.

Article 14 – Prohibition of discrimination

By virtue of Article 14, states must secure the enjoyment of all Convention rights without discrimination on any of the listed grounds.[4] The list is not exhaustive, meaning that discrimination based on disability is forbidden within the sphere of the Convention. Article 14 can only be relied on if the facts of the case bring it within the scope of another Convention

---

1. See *Obermeier v. Austria*, Judgment of 28 June 1990, Series A No. 179.
2. See *Lundevall v. Sweden*, (App. No. 38629/97) and *Salomonsson v. Sweden*, (App. No. 38978/97), judgments of 12 November 2002.
3. *Graeme v. United Kingdom*, Commission decision of 5 February 1990.
4. "sex, race, colour, language, religion, political or other opinion, national or social origin, association with a national minority, property, birth or any other status".

provision. It is not therefore fully autonomous. An example of a case where the discrimination argument succeeded is Koua Poirrez v. France.[1] At issue here was the applicant's entitlement to the special allowance for disabled adults. His application had been refused on the basis of his nationality. In finding a violation of Article 14 (and of Article 1 of Protocol No. 1), the Court attached particular weight to the fact that the benefit was intended for persons with a disability, and cited, for further emphasis, other relevant Council of Europe texts in this domain.

More generally, the Court has ruled that Article 14 is not confined to cases where similar situations are treated differently. It also requires that states treat differently persons whose situations are significantly different,[2] a principle that could well be relied on by a person with a disability.

Furthermore, the Court has affirmed that Article 14 forbids indirect discrimination too.[3]

The scope for raising arguments based on the principle of non-discrimination will be greatly enlarged with the entry into force of Protocol No. 12 to the Convention, which stipulates a fully autonomous right to equality in the enjoyment of any right set forth by law.[4]

As regards the second question namely, whether the state Parties to the Convention have an obligation to take positive measures to assist disabled persons to overcome their problems as much as possible the answer is that the approach of the case law has so far been extremely hesitant. This is up to a point understandable considering that any precedent to the effect of accepting an obligation on the part of the states to provide special facilities in order to solve general problems of disabled persons resulting from their disability will entail an

---

1. No. 40892/98, ECHR 2003-X.
2. *Thlimmenos v. Greece*, [GC], No. 34369/97, ECHR 2000-IV.
3. *Hugh Jordan v. the United Kingdom*, no. 24746/94, judgment of 4 May 2001, ECHR 2001-III (extracts).
4. Opened for signature in November 2000, ten ratifications are needed for the Protocol to take effect. To date, six states have completed ratification.

inestimable burden on the economic capacity of the state concerned.

Several applications have been lodged by disabled persons seeking to establish a positive obligation on state authorities to ensure them increased mobility or autonomy. *In Botta v. Italy,*[1] the applicant, who had a physical disability, complained of the difficulties of gaining access to a private bathing establishment and to a beach. The Court accepted in principle that there could be a duty on the state to take appropriate measures, but there had to be a direct and immediate link between these measures and the private life of the applicant. In this particular case, the scope of the measures requested was too broad and indeterminate. In the later case of *Zehnalová and Zehnal v. the Czech Republic,*[2] the first applicant, who was confined to a wheelchair, complained that many public buildings in her town were inaccessible for her. Although it reiterated the point that Article 8 may imply a duty "in exceptional cases" for the state to take certain steps, the Court found that there was no direct and immediate link to the applicants' private lives.

More recently again, the Court was asked to consider whether a severely physically disabled young man in the Netherlands could invoke Article 8 to demand that he be provided with a robotic arm, without which he would remain totally dependent on others for every need.[3] It accepted that, given his very particular circumstances, the applicant had shown a special link between his demand and the needs of his private life. However, the matter was one that fell within the margin of appreciation of the national authorities, especially in the context of the allocation of limited public funds. Moreover, the Court was wary of setting a precedent. It considered that since the applicant already enjoyed a certain level of public assistance, the state had fulfilled its duty under Article 8.

---

1. *Botta v. Italy*, Judgment of 24 February 1998, Reports of Judgments and Decisions 1998-I.
2. *Zehnalová and Zehnal v. the Czech Republic* (dec.), No. 38621/97, ECHR 2002-V.
3. *Sentges v. Netherlands* (dec), No. 27977/02, not yet reported.

45

It is evident that the case law is reluctant to extend the obligation of the states Parties to the Convention to take positive measures to solve the problems resulting from the disability of a person. In cases where the complaint relates to general problems of indeterminate scope which would cover everything and anything in abstracto which could or could not be of direct significance for the life of a particular disabled person the position of the jurisprudence is in my opinion correct. But one could not exclude an obligation on the part of the state to solve specific problems of a disabled person which are essential for the enjoyment of life in a modern society and are within the financial capacity of the state. I believe that this was in fact the situation in the Botta case and that is why I expressed a dissenting opinion, in the report of the European Commission of Human Rights, where I have stressed *inter alia* the following:

"The personality of individuals cannot be developed in a vacuum. It goes hand in hand with the developments of the social environment. I believe that the positive obligations of the state for an effective protection of the private life or personality of an individual entail the duty to secure to everyone certain minimum rights and facilities to enable the free development of his or her personality in the context of the conditions of social life. ... Things which are essential for the enjoyment of life in a modern society and are intended to be enjoyed through public use (transport, roads, buildings, beaches with facilities, etc.) should be made accessible to every individual to develop freely his personality or to meet the essential needs of his personality.... The Court added that 'this is an area in which the Contracting Parties enjoy a wide margin of appreciation in determining the steps to be taken to ensure compliance with the Convention with due regard to the needs and resources of the community and of individuals'.... However, according to the Italian legislation there is an obligation to insert in the state concessionary contracts (such as in the present case) a provision imposing the duty to the relevant beach establishments to make the necessary arrangements to allow handicapped persons to have access to the beach and to the sea. In enacting the legislation in question; Italy must have taken into account the needs and resources of its community. Consequently, I find that the omission of the competent authorities to enforce the above-mentioned legislation with the result that persons like the applicant were deprived of the possibility to have access to the public facilities of the beach in question amounts to a breach of the positive obligations of the respondent state to ensure an effective protection of the right to respect for the private life of the applicant, contrary to Article 8 of the Convention".

Epilogue

I have tried to show how the Convention has been applied in order to meet the special problems of people with disabilities. Although the Convention was not intended to be an instrument aiming specifically at the solution of such problems, the jurisprudence has evolved in a way as to give particular attention to these problems and take them into account in applying the rights enshrined in the Convention. The big step would have, of course, been to establish through the case-law a principle of an obligation of the States Parties to the Convention to take positive measures to facilitate the disabled persons to overcome as much as possible their problems and enjoy life under better conditions similar, whenever that is feasible, to those applicable to their fellow human beings who do not have any disability. The legal scope of the Convention makes this step difficult but not impossible. The provisions of Article 2 (right to life) Article 3 (prohibition of torture and inhuman and degrading treatment) and Article 8 (right to respect of private life) may be interpreted in a progressive and liberal manner so as to establish the necessary conditions for a better, more tolerable life for all those who had the misfortune to suffer from disabilities that affect substantially their quality of life. But there will always be the obstacle of the financial capacity of every state to make this objective a reality.

The ECHR has proved that it is particularly sensitive to human problems and has adjusted accordingly on many occasions

47

and in different contexts the interpretation and application of the rights safeguarded by the Convention. The Convention is being developed taking into account the needs of human beings and the interest shown by the people themselves as regards such needs. Therefore the demonstration and expression of a constant interest by society and the persons concerned as well as a co-operation on the part of the High Contracting Parties to the Convention is essential for the achievement of an improved and more extensive protection of the rights and dignity of people with disabilities. The Convention cannot, of course, solve all the problems of the disabled persons but it can certainly contribute greatly to their alleviation.

The rights of persons with disabilities under the European Social Charter

Mr Regis BRILLAT
Head of the Social Charter Secretariat
Directorate General of Human Rights
Council of Europe

Abstract

A "natural complement" to the European Convention on Human Rights, the European Social Charter is playing an increasing role in the European legal system. The rights set down in the 1948 Universal Declaration of Human Rights are, in practice, maintained through these texts, which are binding throughout the continent of Europe.

Among the rights laid down in the European Social Charter, are:

– under Article 15, the right of persons with disabilities to independence, social integration and participation in the life of the community,

– under Articles 7 and 17, the right of children and young persons to social, legal and economic protection,

– under Article 9, the right to vocational guidance,

– under Article 10, the right to vocational training,

– under Article 11, the right to protection of health.

A reporting system and a collective complaints procedure are used to monitor observance of the rights for which the European Social Charter provides.

These procedures have enabled the European Committee of Social Rights to detail the scope of the rights which exist under the Charter and to indicate to states what measures they need to take to observe these. In this context, the committee draws dynamically and resolutely on the case-law of the European Court of Human Rights when interpreting the rights for which the European Social Charter provides. It thus both illustrates and implements the fundamental principles of the indivisibility and interdependence of human rights.

The European Committee on Social Rights delivered its decision on 4 November 2003 on the merits of the collective complaint by Autism Europe against France, detailing the interpretation of these rights and the ensuing obligations for states.

Presentation

I would like to thank the organisers of this conference for inviting me to talk about the European Social Charter, it is still too little known and sometimes misunderstood, so it needs to be talked about as often as possible, particularly at conferences on the subject of human rights.

Before telling you precisely what rights it secures to children with disabilities, I would like to give you a brief introduction to the Charter and describe how its supervisory mechanism works.

What is the Social Charter?

The European Social Charter is a Council of Europe treaty, under which states undertake to guarantee certain human rights to their population in addition to those enshrined in the European Convention on Human Rights. It was adopted in

1961 and underwent a complete revision in 1996, which changed both the rights it sets forth and the supervisory mechanisms designed to ensure that these rights are effectively respected by the states parties.

The Social Charter has been ratified thus far by 36 of the 46 member states of the Council of Europe, and other ratifications are on the way. Very soon therefore, practically all of the Council of Europe member states will be bound by the Social Charter. This will contribute to the realisation of one of the goals set for our organisation by its Statute, namely the protection of human rights.

The rights guaranteed by the Charter affect all people every day of their lives, as they relate to significant areas of personal and community life, particularly to housing, health, education, employment, legal protection, social protection and the movement of persons, and, more specifically, to the situation of aliens and the absence of discrimination.

It forms a natural complement to the European Convention on Human Rights and is increasingly a part of the European legal system. There is indeed, ever more perceptibly, a continuum of rights, with binding rules guaranteeing throughout Europe the rights enshrined in the Universal Declaration of Human Rights of 1948.

Certain articles of the European Social Charter relate directly or indirectly to the subject of our conference today. These are:

- Article 15, guaranteeing the right of persons with disabilities to independence, social integration and participation in the life of the community;

- Articles 7 and 17, guaranteeing the rights of children and young persons to social, legal and economic protection;

- Article 9, guaranteeing the right to vocational guidance;

- Article 10, guaranteeing the right to vocational training; and

- Article 11, guaranteeing the right to protection of health.

This short list gives an idea of the richness of the Social Charter and the broad range of situations it covers and individual rights it protects.

However, as was so clearly revealed in the previous speakers' statements, one of the Council of Europe's distinctive characteristics is that it does not regard it as enough to draw up a list or catalogue of rights; it must also set up mechanisms with the purpose and the effect of ensuring that these rights are respected in practice, that is to say that governments are honouring their commitments and individuals fully enjoying their rights.

How does the supervisory mechanism ensure that the rights set forth in the European Social Charter are respected?

A reporting system

As under many international treaties, states have a duty under the Social Charter to report regularly on its implementation, focusing in particular on measures taken to ensure that rights are effectively respected. The system has been operating for nearly forty years and has given rise to thorough investigative work on the real situation in each country concerned. The European Committee of Social Rights, which comprises 15 independent, impartial experts, has the task of ruling whether or not the situation in the country is in conformity with the Charter. All its findings are published and made available on the Council of Europe's web site.

A collective complaints procedure

Furthermore, since the reform, there has been a collective complaints procedure allowing trade unions, employers' organisations and non-governmental organisations to take their case to the European Committee of Social Rights if they believe that a situation is not in conformity with the Social Charter.

The procedure – which was introduced in 1998 – is not yet fully up to speed. It is still too early to draw any definitive conclusions about its contribution to the protection of Charter

51

rights or its exact operating methods, still less about its future. However, enough experience has been derived from a significant number of complaints (28 to date) for a close observer to identify some key features of the system. I am sure that it is largely because the procedure exists and has already had occasion to deal with cases in the area of concern to us here that the conference organisers asked me to speak here today.

The collective complaints procedure has enabled groups (unions and NGOs) to appropriate the treaty, refer to it in their day-to-day activities and understand how important a role it can play in the life of individuals. It has given the European Committee of Social Rights an opportunity to clarify the scope of Charter rights and inform governments of the measures they should be taking to ensure that these rights are respected. The Committee works with energy and determination in this area, drawing on the case-law of the European Court of Human Rights when interpreting Social Charter rights, and hence reflecting and implementing the fundamental principles of the indivisibility and interdependence of human rights.

What then is the substantive content of the rights guaranteed by the Charter for children with disabilities?

Firstly – and although this is an obvious point it may be worth reiterating – children with disabilities enjoy all the rights guaranteed in the European Social Charter.

I will give only one example of this, namely the right to health provided for by Article 11. For this right to be respected, governments are required to set up a health care system that is accessible to all in order to keep people in the best possible state of health in the light of current scientific knowledge. Clearly, one of the essential components of this right is the right to a healthy environment.

Furthermore, special attention is paid to such children, as the rights in the Charter must be secured without discrimination. Article E of the revised Charter of 1996 prohibits discrimination, and the European Committee of Social Rights has confirmed that, although disabilities are not expressly mentioned in the list of grounds for discrimination proscribed in Article E, they are quite adequately covered by the term "other status".

This is particularly in keeping with the spirit and the letter of the political declaration adopted at the end of the 2nd European Conference of Ministers responsible for Integration Policies for People with Disabilities (Malaga, May 2003), in which it was reiterated that the appropriate context for the development of a European policy in this area was one of non-discrimination and human rights.

This prohibition of discrimination on the ground of disability is very wide-ranging, covering both direct discrimination and all forms of indirect discrimination, which can be revealed by inappropriate handling of certain situations or unequal access to various collective benefits between persons placed in such situations and other citizens. In this connection, the Committee has noted that the wording of Article E is very close to that of Article 14 of the European Convention of Human Rights, so it has interpreted it in the light of the European Court of Human Rights' case-law. In its interpretation of Article 14, the Court has pointed out in particular that the underlying principle of equality implies not only that persons in the same situation should be treated in the same way, but also that persons in different situations should be treated differently. In the Thlimmenos v. Greece judgment ([GC], No 34369/97, ECHR 2000-IV, §44), the Court states:

"The right not to be discriminated against in the enjoyment of the rights guaranteed under the Convention is also violated when States without an objective and reasonable justification fail to treat differently persons whose situations are significantly different."

The European Committee of Social Rights has echoed this idea as follows:

"In other words, human difference in a democratic society should not only be viewed positively but should be responded

53

to with discernment in order to ensure real and effective equality."

In addition to full enjoyment of all rights without discrimination, the Social Charter guarantees specific rights to children with disabilities.

The organisers have asked me to spend a little time explaining a collective complaint lodged against France by a non-governmental organisation, Autism Europe. In describing this collective complaint and the decision of the European Committee of Social Rights on its merits, therefore, I will take the opportunity to set out the specific rights enjoyed by children with disabilities, as the interpretation in the Committee's decision of 4 November 2003 adds to and fleshes out the interpretation previously made during examinations of national reports.

The complainant organisation alleged that the situation was not in conformity with the European Social Charter and, in particular, with Articles 17 and 15, because provision was not always made for autistic children owing, inter alia, to the unavailability of special education institutions and services, the inadequacy of early intervention processes, the inadequacy of mainstream education and deficiencies in special education. The result, according to Autism Europe, was that autistic children and adults were too frequently sent to hospital.

The European Committee of Social Rights is responsible for interpreting the European Social Charter, and, when asked to determine, with regard to the case in question, the precise nature and content of states' positive obligations in this matter, it interpreted Articles 15 and 17 of the Charter in the way I shall now set out. It goes without saying that this interpretation applies to all the states that have ratified the Charter.

(a) Right to education and training

All people with disabilities, particularly children, have the right to education. The combined effect of Articles 15§1 and 17 of the Social Charter is to guarantee them the right to be integrated into the education and training facilities available in their country. To facilitate this integration, governments are required, among other things, to train and assist teachers and other education staff and make buildings accessible.

As part of its regular examination of reports by states, the Committee has questioned governments on the provision made for disabled children in school curricula and the funds allocated to integration.

It is a requirement for special educational establishments to be set up, but these are expected to be used only when it is impossible for children to be integrated into the general system. Special schools must be run by the education authorities, regularly inspected and prepare pupils for recognised qualifications that can lead to engagement in paid employment.

Article 15 of the Social Charter was substantially altered when the whole Charter was revised in the early 1990s. In its 1961 version, Article 15 provided for the right of disabled persons – including children – to suitable vocational training and special employment conditions. The revision of the Charter placed the right to social integration and participation in the life of the community at the heart of the article. The change was prompted by a – now generally recognised – socially inclusive philosophy, which the European Committee of Social Rights had borne in mind as far as the text of the Charter allowed. The revision of the Charter now allows it to go much further, as Article 15 now covers many questions outside the world of work and work-related concerns.

In its decision of 4 November 2003, the Committee stated in this connection that Article 15 of the revised Charter – relating to children, young people and adults – reflected:

"a profound shift of values in all European countries over the past decade away from treating [people with disabilities] as objects of pity and towards respecting them as equal citizens – an approach that the Council of Europe contributed to promote, with the adoption by the Committee of Ministers of Recommendation (92) 6 of 1992 on a coherent policy for people with disabilities. The underlying vision of Article 15 is

one of equal citizenship for persons with disabilities and, fittingly, the primary rights are those of 'independence, social integration and participation in the life of the community'. Securing a right to education for children and others with disabilities plays an obviously important role in advancing these citizenship rights. This explains why education is now specifically mentioned in the revised Article 15 and why such an emphasis is placed on achieving that education 'in the framework of general schemes, wherever possible'. It should be noted that Article 15 applies to all persons with disabilities regardless of the nature and origin of their disability and irrespective of their age. It thus clearly covers both children and adults with autism."

With regard to Article 17 – which relates only to children and young people, not to adults – the Committee stated: "Article 17 is predicated on the need to ensure that children and young persons grow up in an environment which encourages the full development of their personality and of their physical and mental capacities". This approach is just as important for children with disabilities as it is for others and arguably more in circumstances where the effects of ineffective or untimely intervention are ever likely to be undone. The Committee views Article 17, which deals more generally, inter alia, with the right to education for all, as also embodying the modern approach of mainstreaming. Article 17§1, in particular, requires the establishment and maintenance of sufficient and adequate institutions and services for the purpose of education."

(b) Application of these rights

Another important point about the decision of 4 November 2003 is that the European Committee of Social Rights refers in detail – in an almost pedagogical manner – to the arrangements that governments must make to apply the rights in question despite the extremely difficult circumstances.

Its application of these principles prompted the Committee to rule that the situation in France was not in conformity with the Charter.

In connection with this case, the Committee of Ministers – which has the task of following up decisions of the European Committee of Social Rights – adopted a resolution on 10 March 2004, in which it:

"1. Takes note of the statement made by the respondent Government indicating that the French Government undertakes to bring the situation into conformity with the Revised Charter and that measures are being taken in this respect (see Appendix to this resolution);

2. Looks forward to France reporting that, at the time of the submission of the next report concerning the relevant provisions of the Revised European Social Charter, the situation has improved."

Conclusion

In conclusion it can be said that the significant advances brought about by the European Social Charter should not be regarded as the end of the road. In the way it was devised and the manner in which it is interpreted, the Charter is a dynamic instrument destined to continue along the difficult but necessary path of protecting economic and social rights as human rights.

The ratification and then the entry into force of the Constitution of the European Union, which includes not only civil and political, but also economic and social rights, brings the question of the possible accession of the European Union to the European Social Charter back onto the agenda. It draws our attention once again to the importance of giving thought to the possibility of introducing social rights into the European Convention on Human Rights or of introducing a procedure for individual complaints into the European Social Charter system.

The Third Summit of Heads of State and Government of the Council of Europe, to be held in Warsaw next May, could provide an opportunity to agree on a framework and timetable for further discussion on this subject.

INTRODUCTION TO THE THEMES

The draft UN comprehensive and integral international convention on the protection and promotion of the rights and dignity of persons with disabilities

Mr Arnt HOLTE
Chairman of the Norwegian Federation of Organisations
of Disabled People (FFO),
Member of the Norwegian delegation to the UN,
Ad hoc Committee

I would first like to express my appreciation for being invited to take part in this seminar in order to talk about the work involving the UN Convention. My name is Arnt Holte, and I am the President of the umbrella organisation for disabled people in Norway. Its members comprise sixty-six different disability organisations, and these organisations include approximately 270,000 persons.

I would like to share with you some of my background. I am disabled myself, born blind, and I have worked for three different disability organisations in Norway.

I would like to emphasise that the Norwegian authorities place great importance on maintaining a good relationship with disability organisations. I was invited to participate in the Council of Europe's Ministerial Conference on Disability in Malaga, Spain, in May 2003. This was the basis for further discussions with the Norwegian Government, and I was invited to participate in the Norwegian delegation to the Fourth Ad Hoc Meeting on a Convention for Rights of disabled people, which was held in New York in August-September 2004.

When we now discuss disabilities with a human rights perspective, it is important that we, as a basis for the discussion, stress the fact that disabled people are discriminated against. If that is not established, it will be difficult to achieve a special convention that will secure and protect the rights of disabled people.

Why is it important that disabled people themselves participate in the work? When a convention is formed, it is important that disabled people themselves participate in the work. Our background includes a level of competence that is essential when this work will be implemented. One would never have developed a convention for women without having the women play an integral part in the work. My experience from the meeting in New York revealed that such relevant background was important, and that it influenced the details of its contents, as well as raising important questions of principle.

Challenges in the work ahead

In my judgement, we are now facing some great challenges. At this time I would like to point out that this convention will secure for disabled people equal access to both the civil and political human rights, and social, economic and cultural human rights. The process of securing economic, cultural and social rights will naturally be realised gradually, but civil and political human rights should be in place.

Another element, which is also important, is that this convention will not provide new rights, but will secure equal rights. But there will always be those who will attempt to establish new rights.

In addition, it is a fact that the situation varies greatly from country to country. It is therefore a huge job that must be done in order to achieve consensus on solutions.

There are other challenges that can be mentioned - how international co-operation should influence the states' implementation of equal rights. There is also disagreement on how in future the work should be carried out.

I think that this work is important in order to secure human rights for disabled people in the future. I would also like to

60

point out that the process itself is of great importance. It increases the focus on the situation of disabled people, and the co-operation between governments and organisations of disabled people, and in the process increasing the understanding to find solutions.

In closing I would like to thank you for having afforded me this opportunity to put forward these points of view, as well as to thank the Norwegian Government for involving disabled people. "Nothing about us without us" covers this process.

Comments on the draft UN disability convention

Mr Carlos SALAZAR
Deputy Permanent Observer
Permanent Mission of Mexico to the Council of Europe

It is an honour for me to participate, on behalf of the Mexican Government, in this event organised by the Council of Europe, in order to discuss with you the reasons which prompted the Mexican Government to propose the drafting and negotiation of a binding legal instrument on persons with disabilities. As you are aware, in September 2001, Mr Vicente Fox Quesada, President of the United Mexican States, submitted a proposal to the United Nations General Assembly for the establishment of an ad hoc committee to draft a Convention to Promote and Protect the Rights and Dignity of Persons with Disabilities, based on a holistic approach encompassing provisions on social development, human rights and non-discrimination. I should like to share with you some of the reasons behind this proposal:

a.   The Universal Declaration of Human Rights proclaims that all human beings are born free and equal in dignity and rights and that everyone is entitled to all the rights set forth therein, without distinction of any kind.

b.   Worldwide, there are currently over 600 million people with disabilities, which is equivalent to 10% of the world population, and 80% of these live in the developing countries. Year after year, armed conflicts, widespread violence, the use of anti-personnel land mines, natural disasters and accidents increase the number of people with disabilities, thereby further exacerbating the already unfavourable conditions in which these people live.

c.   The efforts undertaken by the international community in the last 20 years to address the needs of persons with disabilities and secure their full and effective participation have been insufficient and fragmented. They have not succeeded in redressing the constant violations of the human rights of persons with disabilities or in eliminating the prejudice, stereotyping and discrimination with which they are faced.

d.   The importance of moving ahead with the gradual development of international law and filling a large legal vacuum. In this connection, it is important to remember that the majority of existing instruments addressing the issue of disability are not legally binding (for example, the Standard Rules of 1993). Furthermore, the existing standards are scattered across different instruments, deal with very limited aspects (for example, the International Labour Organization's Vocational Rehabilitation and Employment (Disabled Persons) Convention, No.159 of 1983) or are not sufficiently specific, not to mention the lack of provisions concerning non-discrimination on grounds of disability.

e.   An instrument aimed at a specific group will serve to focus attention on aspects and situations which are less visible under general human rights instruments, as is the case with the Convention for the Elimination of All Forms of Discrimination against Women or the Convention on the Rights of the Child.

f.   It is particularly important in this context to translate the internationally recognised civil, political, economic, social and cultural rights into practical terms in order to eliminate the specific barriers facing people with disabilities and thus to secure the recognition and effective exercise of all their human rights and encourage a broad commitment to providing them with improved access and equality of opportunity in the different spheres of life.

g.   The convention will help to build awareness of disability issues and move ahead with the adoption and/or amendment of national laws in many countries, in order to incorporate the progress made in the area of disability.

h.   Last but not least, the convention will meet a legitimate demand on the part of international civil society.

Since the Ad Hoc Committee was set up in 2001, various decisions have been taken that have helped to consolidate this important process and on which I should like to comment briefly in view of their relevance to, and impact on, the work in progress.

1.   The Ad Hoc Committee set up by the General Assembly is open to the participation of all member states and observers of the United Nations.

2.   In an unprecedented move, the General Assembly decided to authorise the participation of non-governmental organisations in the work of the Ad Hoc Committee. To facilitate the participation of experts and representatives from developing countries, it was decided to set up a fund for voluntary contributions.

3.   In the same way, the Secretary General was asked to take measures, as needed and within existing resources, to facilitate the participation of persons with disabilities in the meetings and deliberations of the Ad Hoc Committee. This included facilitating their access to UN premises and providing documents in formats readable by persons with visual disabilities.

4.   The Ad Hoc Committee's work has been enriched by the many contributions from governments, meeting recommendations, expert workshops and regional seminars; there has been input from United Nations bodies and specialised agencies; and there has been input from intergovernmental bodies, from national institutions and from non-governmental organisations. It should be mentioned that the committee has received seven complete draft texts of the convention, including the text originally submitted by the Mexican Government, whose main purpose was to stimulate and enrich the discussions of the Ad Hoc Committee.

63

5.   The Ad Hoc Committee also derived material for its work from the round tables and expert panels convened to address issues relating to the nature, structure, components and monitoring system of the convention, the principles of non-discrimination and equality from the perspective of persons with disabilities, and new approaches to the definition of disability.

6.   In this process, it is important to mention the co-operation established between the Office of the High Commissioner for Human Rights and the Secretariat's Department of Economic and Social Affairs to support the work of the Ad Hoc Committee.

7.   Lastly, the General Assembly adopted a resolution in December 2003 in which, among other things, the member states and observers are encouraged to participate actively in the work of the Ad Hoc Committee in order to ensure that a draft convention is submitted to the General Assembly for adoption as a matter of priority, and it was decided that the Ad Hoc Committee would start the negotiations on the text of the convention at its third session, based on the text prepared by the joint Working Group consisting of 27 governmental representatives appointed by the regional groups, 12 representatives of non-governmental organisations and one representative of national human rights institutions, which met in New York in January 2004.

Results of the meeting of the Ad Hoc Committee's Working Group (January 2004, New York)

The group's mandate was, while taking due account of the many contributions received, to prepare and present a draft text to serve as a basis for the negotiations at the Ad Hoc Committee's third session held in New York from 24 May to 4 June 2004. To facilitate the group's work, the Chair submitted a proposal for the structure and text of the convention and the Secretariat produced a compilation based on the 33 contributions received to date by the Ad Hoc Committee.

As a result of this work, the group adopted a detailed draft of the convention which consists of a preamble and 25 articles and is geared to the protection of all internationally recognised human rights (civil, political, economic, social and cultural) and not based solely on non-discrimination. The text also identifies specific measures to secure to persons with disabilities the full enjoyment of their human rights and enable them to participate in all spheres of life and become full members of society.

Given that the group's mandate was not to negotiate a draft convention, the draft reflects the basic agreement reached on the issues to be included in a legally binding instrument and includes various footnotes drawing the Ad Hoc Committee's attention to those issues which require further analysis in view of their complexity and the differing views expressed.

Third and fourth sessions (May-June and August-September 2004, New York)

In 2004, the Ad Hoc Committee met twice for a period of ten working days. The topics currently under discussion in the Ad Hoc Committee include: the general obligations of states, including the gradual implementation of some of the rights contained in the convention; whether or not it is necessary to have definitions and terms of reference; the legal capacity of persons with disabilities and the assistance which they can and should be given in this regard; health, employment and social security issues; medical treatment and forced institutionalisation; inclusive or special education; special or compensatory measures; collecting statistics and data without interfering in people's private lives; the establishment of monitoring machinery and the role of international co-operation in the context of the convention.

Among other things, the committee has also considered whether it is necessary to strengthen some of the aspects of the text relating to equality of opportunity, and how persons with disabilities can participate in the life of the community, live independently and take up an economically active role. Another important point is the need to ensure that the broad nature of the convention is properly reflected in the preamble and the general articles, such as those stating its purpose or setting out principles and general obligations.

Final remarks

It is an unfortunate fact that persons with disabilities are subjected to constant violations of their human rights and are faced with prejudice, stereotyping and discrimination, in addition to being confronted with other obstacles of a physical, social and cultural nature. It is against this background that the international community has taken up the major challenge of making progress on the drafting of a single instrument protecting and promoting all the human rights of persons with disabilities. The work done in the Ad Hoc Committee over the last three years has made it possible to achieve a consensus on the necessity and importance of having a legally binding instrument for persons with disabilities, thus making it possible to overcome the problems that characterised the discussions in the early stages of the committee's work.

The many contributions received by the Ad Hoc Committee show the interest which the topic has aroused within the international community and the importance of ensuring that the convention is a pioneering instrument reflecting the changes in the disability field over the last few years, covering all human rights, including civil, political, economic, social and cultural rights, and meeting the different needs of persons suffering from different kinds of disability. In the opinion of the Mexican Government, an instrument for the 21st century will require monitoring machinery and should promote co-operation and information exchange between states, as well as promoting technical co-operation and best practices in order to help states to honour their commitments.

We currently have a draft convention text which forms an excellent basis for continuing the work undertaken by the Ad Hoc Committee. The Mexican Government is convinced that at the Ad Hoc Committee's forthcoming meetings in 2005 it will be possible to make progress on the negotiation of a strong convention text that can be adopted by the Assembly as a matter of priority and will have a positive impact on the lives of millions of disabled people the world over. This will only be possible with the firm commitment and political will of the member states and other stakeholders.

Mexico attaches great importance to the participation of disability experts and non-governmental organisations in the work of the Ad Hoc Committee as it is convinced that the only way to produce the best possible instrument for protecting and promoting all the human rights of persons with disabilities is to take into consideration the contributions, knowledge and experience of all the stakeholders, including the main beneficiaries. We shall continue to encourage extensive participation by non-governmental organisations and experts in this process.

I should like to take this opportunity to appeal to the ministers and government representatives present here to become directly involved in the negotiations on this international instrument. I am sure that the work of the Council of Europe and the action plan on disability, which is to be discussed at this meeting, can make an enormous contribution to the work and negotiations in progress in the UN Ad Hoc Committee.

Lastly, it remains for me to thank you for this invitation and reiterate Mexico's determination to bring this initiative to a successful conclusion.

Thank you.

At the current stage, the draft convention text consists of the following sections and articles:

Preamble

Article 1:	Purpose
Article 2:	General principles
Article 3:	Definitions
Article 4:	General obligations
Article 5:	Promotion of positive attitudes to persons with disabilities
Article 6:	Statistics and data collection
Article 7:	Equality and non-discrimination
Article 8:	Right to life
Article 9:	Equal recognition as a person before the law
Article 10:	Liberty and security of the person
Article 11:	Freedom from torture or cruel, inhuman or degrading treatment or punishment

Article 12:   Freedom from violence and abuse
Article 13:   Freedom of expression and opinion, and access to information
Article 14:   Respect for privacy, the home and the family
Article 15:   Living independently and being included in the community
Article 16:   Children with disabilities
Article 17:   Education
Article 18:   Participation in political and public life
Article 19:   Accessibility
Article 20:   Personal mobility
Article 21:   Right to health and rehabilitation
Article 22:   Right to work
Article 23:   Social security and an adequate standard of living
Article 24:   Participation in cultural life, recreation, leisure and sport
Article 24bis: International co-operation
Article 25:   Monitoring

The draft Council of Europe Disability Action Plan

Mr J. Hans SLUITER
Chairman of the Council of Europe
Disability Action Plan Drafting Group
Senior Policy Adviser
Disabled Persons Policy Directorate
Ministry of Health, Welfare and Sports, The Hague
The Netherlands

Abstract

The pioneering Council of Europe Recommendation No. R (92)6 on a coherent policy for people with disabilities, result of the first Council of Europe Ministerial Conference on disability held in 1991, has guided the course of thinking on disability policies in the last decade. A fundamental shift took place in the perception of disability; from stressing limitations and disabilities to abilities and social capacities: a paradigm shift from patient to citizen.

In May 2003, during the Second European Conference of Ministers responsible for integration policies for people with disabilities in Malaga, Ministers adopted the Malaga Ministerial Declaration ("Progressing towards full participation as citizens") and recommended the elaboration of a new European policy framework on disability for the next decade. In September 2003 the Committee of Ministers of the Council of Europe regarded the drafting of a Council of Europe Disability Action Plan, applicable to all member states, as a priority.

The Council of Europe Disability Action Plan seeks to translate the aims of the Council of Europe into a pan-European policy framework on disability for the next decade. Basic elements of this framework are:

– the mission and strategic goals,
– the key action lines,
– relevant cross-cutting issues and principles,
– implementation strategies,
– monitoring mechanisms.

Member states, and national disabled persons' organisations (DPOs) represented by the European Disability Forum (EDF), are actively involved in the drafting process.

The mission of the Action Plan is to establish a purposeful policy framework aimed at the protection, social inclusion, and the improvement of the quality of life of people with disabilities on a pan-European scale. Following a human rights perspective, the Disability Action Plan promotes the elimination of all forms of discrimination, with a special focus on children, disabled women and people with disabilities in need of a high level of support. The Council of Europe Disability Action Plan has a broad scope and encompasses all key policy issues and key areas of the daily life of people with disabilities e.g. community living, education, employment, social protection, a barrier free environment. These key issues and areas are duly reflected in the action lines. The overarching theme of the

69

action lines is the enhancement of accessibility in the broadest sense: access to social rights, provisions and services and the environment. General issues and fundamental principles cross-cutting the action lines are highlighted. The Disability Action Plan opens the way for a viable course of action in all Council of Europe member states. Due account is taken of the different stages of development in various member states.

The Council of Europe will facilitate implementation of the Action Plan through providing positive assistance to the member states by giving advice, information and making recommendations. To get actionable information concerning the progress and impact of the Council of Europe Disability Action Plan, it is necessary to develop effective monitoring mechanisms. Monitoring mechanisms must be especially focused on identifying barriers to equal treatment and full participation and the effects of mainstreaming.

Presentation

First of all I would like to thank the Norwegian Chairmanship for its invitation to participate in this conference on human rights, disability and children. It is a great pleasure to be here to day and an honour to have the opportunity of addressing this important conference.

I would like to give you a general overview of the state of play of the Council of Europe Disability Action Plan. First of all I will touch upon some important developments and historical events that are relevant with a view to the genesis and the current elaboration of the Action Plan. Then I will highlight the mission, the key action lines and relevant cross-cutting issues. And finally I will tell you something about implementation and monitoring mechanisms.

However you should be aware of the fact that the Action Plan is not yet completed. The drafting process is in full swing and the outcome of this conference will also feed in this process. So this is a story about work in progress and a lot of hard work is still ahead! Now, let's start with a brief retrospective.

70

From patient to citizen

The past decades were characterised by changes in the perception of disability. A fundamental shift took place from stressing disabilities, the medical model, via a model underpinning functional abilities, to a social and human rights model aimed at full citizenship. The paradigm shift from patient to citizen!

In 1991 the first Council of Europe Ministerial Conference on disability took place. This conference led to the adoption of the innovative Recommendation No. R (92)6 on a coherent policy for people with disabilities. In 2003, the European Year of People with Disabilities, the second Council of Europe Ministerial Conference was held in Malaga. The Malaga conference, like the first ministerial conference, was a pivotal point in developing Council of Europe disability strategies; strategies to progress towards full citizenship and to raise awareness that disability - in spite of the progress being made - is still an issue of concern in all European countries.

In Malaga the ministers recommended the elaboration of a new European policy framework on disability for the next decade. They also welcomed the initiative to extend the activities of the Committee on the Rehabilitation and Integration of People with disabilities (CD-P-RR) to all Council of Europe member states. In September 2003 the Committee of Ministers of the Council of Europe regarded the drafting of a Disability Action Plan applicable to all member states as a priority. The Action Plan seeks to translate the aims of the Council of Europe into a European policy framework on disability for the next decade.

Basic elements of this framework are:

– mission and strategic goals

– key action lines

– relevant cross-cutting issues and principles

– implementation strategies

– monitoring mechanisms

71

The drafting process started at the 26th session of the CD-P-RR in October 2003. A Working Group was established to elaborate the Action Plan. This Working Group is assisted by a Drafting Group, which takes care of reviewing and editing successive draft versions of the Action Plan. During the 27th meeting of the extended CD-P-RR in Bucharest in September 2004, draft version 6 of the Action Plan was discussed. Member states are actively involved in the drafting process by participating in the groups just mentioned and - more importantly - by submitting draft texts on the various issues.

The Action Plan advocates the role of Disabled Persons Organisations as a source of expert knowledge and sees them as competent partners in policy development. So the European Disability Forum, representing national Disabled Persons Organisations, plays an important and active role in the elaboration of the Council of Europe Action Plan. Now let's look at the structure and content of the Action Plan in more detail.

Mission

The mission of the Action Plan is to establish a viable pan-European policy framework aimed at the protection, social inclusion, and improvement of the quality of life of people with disabilities. From a human rights perspective, the Action Plan aims to promote the elimination of all forms of discrimination, with a special focus on children, disabled women and people with disabilities in need of a high level of support. This mission includes the protection of human rights, reform and main-streaming of governmental policies, institutional restructuring and quality improvement. This is - if I may say so - no mean feat!

Action lines

As we have seen, the Council of Europe Action Plan has a broad scope and encompasses all key policy issues and key areas of the daily life of people with disabilities. These key issues and areas are duly reflected in the action lines. The overarching theme of the action lines is the enhancement of

accessibility in the broadest sense. General issues and fundamental principles crosscutting these action lines, for example
children with disabilities, are also highlighted in the plan. But
the action lines are the core of the Action Plan.

The action lines are pertaining to: community living, a barrier
free environment and accessible transport, health care, education and employment, participation in cultural life and political
life, information, communication and research, social and
legal protection, safeguarding against abuse and, last but not
least, awareness-raising.

As you will understand, it is impossible to go into the details of
each of the action lines. But I will try to highlight and summa-
rize the main points for you.

Opportunities for full participation and inclusion are first of all
created by living in the community. The shift from supply-led
institutional care to consumer driven service provision, cleared
the way for community based services. Equitable access to
these services should be facilitated by an independent, individual and professional assessment of needs.

A barrier-free environment and accessible transport play a key
role in the daily life of all people with disabilities who live or
wish to live in the community, and in particular for families
with a disabled child. Stressing community living may imply
starting a process of institutional reform and restructuring.
When alternative and adequate community based services are
in place, institutions can be phased out. However this should
not rule out sheltered housing and supported living arrangements in the community. Many disabled people living in the
community will require health care and rehabilitation services
to maintain their independence and improve the quality of
their life. In this regard it is important that health care professionals should focus more on the social model of disability.

Education and employment are basic elements to ensure
social inclusion as well as personal and economic independence. Education covers all life stages; it is about life-long
learning. Participation in mainstream education is not only

important for children with disabilities but also for their non-disabled peers. Employment is a key element for the social inclusion and independence of disabled people. Vocational guidance can help people with disabilities to find jobs or activities for which they are best suited. Supported employment is also needed to help disabled people who cannot find a regular job. But man cannot live by work alone! To have a complete social life and be included in society, people with disabilities must also be able to participate in social, cultural and political activities. In this regard, access to information and communication technology is a key condition for full participation in society. So it is imperative that public and private providers of information and communication technologies take into account the needs of people with disabilities. People with disabilities need social and legal protection, including protection against discrimination for reasons of disability and social security. In this respect society also has the duty to prevent and to protect people against acts of abuse and violence, because the rate of acts of violence and abuse committed against disabled people is considerably higher than the rate for the general population.

Public awareness is needed to back up legal and social protection and to increase a better understanding of the needs and rights of people with disabilities in society. Research, data collection and analysis are essential to design and implement well informed and effective policies. But attitudes do not change automatically or spontaneously. Real attitudinal change will only take place when stereo typing and stigmatization are replaced by a positive image of people with disabilities. Therefore raising awareness is a key issue that underpins the whole Action Plan.

Cross-cutting issues

Now let's look more closely at the relevant issues and principles that are cross-cutting the action lines. In the Action Plan, as it stands now, the following cross-cutting issues and principles are elaborated: Children with disabilities, people with disabilities in need of a high level of support, women with disabilities, universal design, quality of services and ageing.

74

For children with disabilities to be able to develop to the best of their abilities the support they receive in childhood will be of great importance for their lives as adults. Intervention and aid at an early stage of a child's development will reduce dependence on specific facilities at a later stage in life. In this sense early intervention and early aid are essential to improve social inclusion of the disabled child as well as the child's family. Children with disabilities should not live in institutions but at home with their parents. But the constant caring for a disabled child at home is demanding and can also have far-reaching financial consequences. Often parents with a disabled child get not enough support or assistance and find themselves very isolated. Mainstream child-care services and respite care can offer relief from the continual stresses of care giving and are needed to lessen the burden of families. For families who cannot represent themselves, advocacy is needed to assist them in finding proper care and support for their disabled child.

People with severe or multiple complex disabilities face all kinds of specific problems. They are often in need of a high level of support. Children and adults with severe or complex disabilities may require intensive assistance and support in a number of domains. They should get services which are geared to meet their specific needs. Full access to these specific services is essential and determines the quality of their lives. Legal and policy initiatives should cater for their needs. Careful planning and appropriate funding is needed for this small, but significantly growing group of individuals.

Although the general situation of people with disabilities has significantly improved, the benefits of positive changes in society are still not equally distributed between women and men with disabilities. Women with disabilities still face multiple obstacles to participate in society due to double discrimination, for example in education, employment and social protection.

Many European countries are already systematically working on improving quality of care provision and service delivery. Quality management is a prerequisite for attaining improvements and quality control. Innovation and making use of information technologies in care and service systems can contribute to a higher quality of long-term care and support services. Quality management in care provision and service delivery also has a significant political dimension. European-wide co-operation and comparison of approach to quality management and quality assurance in similar situations and facilities can enhance quality of service provision and the exchange of best practices.

People with disabilities should play an important role regarding the monitoring and rating of the quality of services on which they are dependent.

Universal design is also an effective way to improve the quality of the environment, services and products. It focuses on the importance of getting the design of the environment, buildings and everyday products right from the start, and not of adapting these things as an afterthought. This is a major topic, because designers can make life very difficult for disabled people. There are still far too many obstacles that impede disabled people to take part in all aspects of society and make use of all its facilities. Therefore user participation is of paramount importance in Universal Design, because users can give designers vital information from a different perspective.

The ageing trend is one of the major social issues of the coming decades. Elderly disabled people will increase in number, bringing an increased need for long-term care and support services. The ageing trend will especially affect intellectually disabled people. Research has shown that ageing processes tend to set in at an earlier age in people with an intellectual handicap. Gradually, they will require care that is more intensive as well as more specialised in many cases. The ageing trend will also make extra demands on the quality of long-term care and service delivery.

Implementation

Now to round off this overview let's move to the issues of implementation and monitoring. The Council of Europe will facilitate implementation of the Action Plan through providing

76

positive assistance to all member states by giving advice, information and making recommendations. Due account is taken of the geographic, economic and social diversity and the different stages of development in various member states.

The Action Plan opens the way for a viable course of action in the member states. But the member states, that's where the action is, or should be! The member states are in the driver's seat! The Action Plan will serve them as a practical tool, a roadmap for action and policy making. The action lines offer guidelines, a toolkit to shape or prioritize and refocus national policies.

The Action Plan can also provide a useful source of inspiration for the private sector, non-governmental organisations, and other international organisations.

An important aspect of implementation is mainstreaming. In Europe today priority is given to mainstream disability policy. People with disabilities should be able to receive the support they need first and foremost within the regular policy frameworks, programmes and services. But we should be aware of the fact that mainstreaming can also be a double-edged word. There is a danger that as result of the fierce competition between all kinds of vested interests, lobbies, and powerful pressure groups in society, the interests of disabled people will be pushed aside or neglected. Because disabled people in with non disabled people still are vulnerable citizens.

Monitoring

It may seem a paradox, but mainstreaming increases the necessity to have an overarching policy framework, an Action Plan, that maintains a focus of attention on disability issues and that will systematically monitor 'the situation on the ground'. Monitoring is necessary to identify sticking points and to signal changing conditions and promising new developments. Monitoring mechanisms must be especially focused on identifying barriers to equal treatment and the effects of mainstreaming.

77

Now within most member states various monitoring mechanisms are already in place. Emphasis should be put on making full use of existing monitoring mechanisms and on recalibrating those mechanisms if necessary. The existence of a focal point within national governments that oversees or co-ordinates disability policies and maintains links with the Council of Europe could facilitate monitoring processes. National Disabled Persons' Organisations (DPOs) are most knowledgeable about the actual situation in their country. They should be actively involved in monitoring and invited to report on regular basis to the government with regard to actual problems and sticking points.

Conclusions

Ladies and gentlemen, I come to the conclusions of my speech. Currently in Europe we are facing great challenges in the social and economic field. However the main objective remains to strive for a society that is accessible to all and that will include people with disabilities. The Action Plan opens the way for collaboration between all member states. It will make it possible to build bridges, to start twinning initiatives between East and West and to exchange expertise, and information on good practices.

The Council of Europe organisation in Strasbourg has a staff of dedicated professionals and is a real treasure house with a wealth of information and expert knowledge about all disability issues. The Council of Europe as a pan-European organisation offers a solid base to set the agenda for the protection of human rights and promoting full citizenship for people with disabilities. The Action Plan is the proper instrument to move this agenda forward in the next decade. This Conference is also a perfect way to strengthen co-operation, to raise awareness and to create broad base support for pressing disability issues.

Madame Chair, ladies and gentlemen, thank you for your attention.

WORKSHOP 1
DEINSTITUTIONALISATION

Chair: Mr Christian KIELLAND, Norway

Challenges of deinstitutionalisation

Prof. Jan TØSSEBRO
Department of Social Work and Health Sciences
Norwegian University of Science & Technology
Trondheim, Norway

Abstract

Disability policy has changed substantially in a number of countries during the last three or four decades. One of the important changes is conceptualised by terms like normalisation, integration, inclusion and deinstitutionalisation – everyone's participation in society. Segregated facilities are downsized and closed, or at least made less segregated. This policy change – and its consequences for people – applies to all age groups, but in accordance with the theme of the conference, the focus of this presentation is children. And with regard to disabled children, a corollary of normalisation is a new division of labour between families, parents and the public.

Even though there is widespread support for the ideals, inclusion policy meets both hesitation and criticism. Some hold that it is unrealistic. One argument is that mainstream services cannot possibly obtain the level of expertise found in specialised units. Another criticism is that we live in societies where exclusion, whether we like it or not, is a reality. If one does not take due account of this, there is a risk that one, with the best intentions, actually causes isolation, loneliness and other kinds of problems for vulnerable children. Some children may need a more protected environment. It is thus reason to ask what happens when inclusion policy is implemented, and particularly how it is experienced where it "hits the ground" – by disabled children and their families. My approach is however not to ask whether it is time to turn back, but as a strategy to identify current challenges. The intention is thus to 1) discuss and describe experiences among families of disabled children and 2) to discuss implementation practices and the main challenges confronting current policy.

The international research literature on desegregation tends to group into two distinct approaches. One addresses effects. It asks, for example, if children learn more, have a more positive self-image etc. in mainstream than segregated settings. Inclusion is seen as a means to reach some other goal, and the question is whether it is efficient or maybe destructive. The other approach is value-based. Everyone's participation is seen as a value in itself. The question is thus if the implementation of "taken for granted" ideals is whole-hearted and brings us closer to the realization of the ideals. Lessons from both points of departure are summarised.

The Scandinavian countries, and in particular Sweden and Norway, are looked upon as some kind of avant-garde in inclusion policy. It is thus of particular interest to address family experiences and current challenges in such countries, in this case Norway. Results from a study following disabled children born 1993-95 as they grow up and a study on intellectually disabled children at school are presented. Themes such as family structure (for instance marriage and divorce, siblings, labour market participation), preschool services, inclusion at school and among peers, family experiences with services and support, etc. are addressed. Even though the "participation of all" policy is summarised as a relative success, a number of challenges are identified such as "pretence implementation" and that the lack of access to services turns the experience of parenting a disabled child into a continuous fight with service agencies.

Presentation

A Norwegian newspaper, autumn 2003: Day 1. The mother of Joakim, 14 years of age, CP, included in a regular class, describes how her son refuses to go to school, how it makes him feel like a failure, that he is isolated, etc. His mother con-cludes that this is not integration, but an exhibition – a freak show, and argues the case of special schools. Day 2. The mother of Lena, 16 years old, Downs' syndrome, describes some of the same problems, but also active engagement and participation in some parts of social life. However, much needs to be done in order to achieve real inclusion.

The main difference between these two stories is not the happy and unhappy one. Both describe problems. It is a dif-ference in interpretation. The mother of Joakim takes the cur-rent school for granted, she observes the shortcomings and concludes that the child needs a more protected and segre-gated environment. The mother of Lena takes the child for granted and argues the case that even though there are prob-lems and shortcomings, one cannot give up the idea that in order to include all children, it is the school that must change..

Introduction

Disability policy has changed in at least two significant ways in a number of countries during the last three to four decades. One of the changes is directly linked to the understanding of disability – moving from an individual/biological understand-ing to a social-ecological model stressing the relation between people and their environment and the fact that the man-made environment is not adapted to the variation of human beings. The consequence is a policy shift focusing on environmental change, accessibility, etc.

The other change, which is the theme of my presentation, is the movement from special segregated services to main-stream, a shift called deinstitutionalisation, integration, nor-malisation, inclusion, etc.. There is a link between the two policy changes, which is more or less expressed in the vision of the UN Year for Disabled People in 1981: Equality and full participation. There is a need to change society in order to make it possible for all to take part – a society for all.

My presentation will concern the deinstitutionalisation part of this development, and in accordance with the theme of the conference I will focus on children. But let me start by pointing out how I see my task: One tends to ask: Did it improve or get worse? Is it better after relocation? In my opinion, a better way to address the question today is to take the reform movement for granted and ask about the problems and mistakes of current services in their own right: the point is not "backwards" comparison but current challenges.

I will however start by looking back – in order to point out that the deinstitutionalisation movement is not just a contemporary fad but more like a master pattern or windmill affecting nearly all parts of the social service system. I will go on to discuss the research on deinstitutionalisation (but very briefly or this presentation would last for hours). And finally, I will address the current challenges from one particular point of departure; that of a country that has gone a fairly long distance down the integration/inclusion road. This will be the only part of my presentation that is not in the birds-eye view.

The politics and practice of deinstitutionalisation

Deinstitutionalisation is a current pervasive trend just like modern, differentiated institutions were a century ago. Stanley Cohen has argued that the development almost looks like a historical "master pattern", affecting nearly all "western" countries, large parts of the social service sector – not at the same time and identically, but in the birds-eye-view. It is a grand overall trend.

Figure 1: No of residents in institutions in Norway, 1945-2000

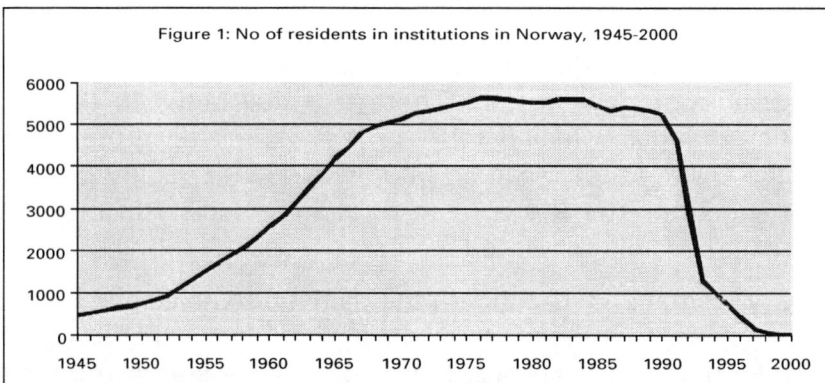

Figure 1: No of residents in institutions in Norway, 1945-2000

Figure 1 on the rise and fall of institutions for intellectually disabled people in Norway is an illustration. The number of places grew rapidly from 1945 to 1970 and declined even more rapidly after 1990. A more exact description of the international movement would start with special schools for sensory-impaired adolescents two centuries ago, subsequently a rapid growth starting with psychiatric institutions from 1850 – and continuing through the 1960s. The first signs of a new era emerged in the middle of the 1950s. The number of beds in US and UK psychiatric hospitals peaked in 1954/55 and in child protection one stressed the benefits of the family and foster home care became the preferred alternative.

Figure 2: Changes in institutionalisation of intellectually disabled people per 1000 citizens, 1980-93 (source: Hatton, Emerson & Kiernan, 1995)

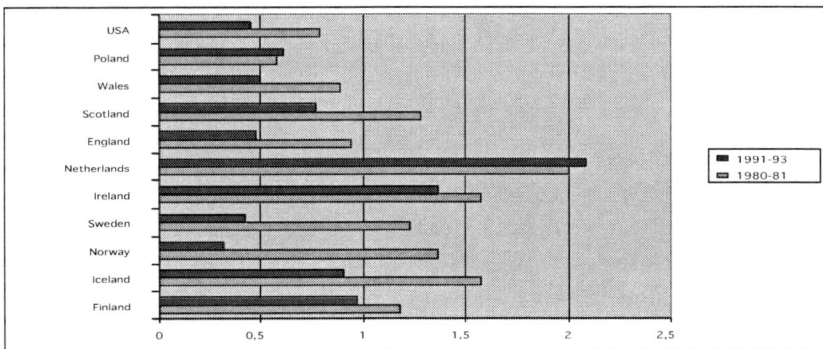

This master pattern takes place in a number of sectors, in a number of countries, but as Figure 2 suggests there are also national differences, which explain deinstitutionalisation of intellectually disabled people during the 1990s.

Even though institutions for intellectually disabled people admitted children (though fewer from the early 1970s), the most important type of institutions for children were the special schools, typically boarding schools. They are downsized and closed in many countries, and although figures are inexact due to differences in definitions of special schools, figure 3 gives some ideas about national differences in the middle of the 1990s in Western Europe. The figure suggests that North

83

West and South Europe have gone further down the road towards integration, whereas Central Europe has changed less.

Figure 3: Pupils in segregated schools/classes in 14 European countries. 1996. Percentage of all children. Source: Vislie 2003

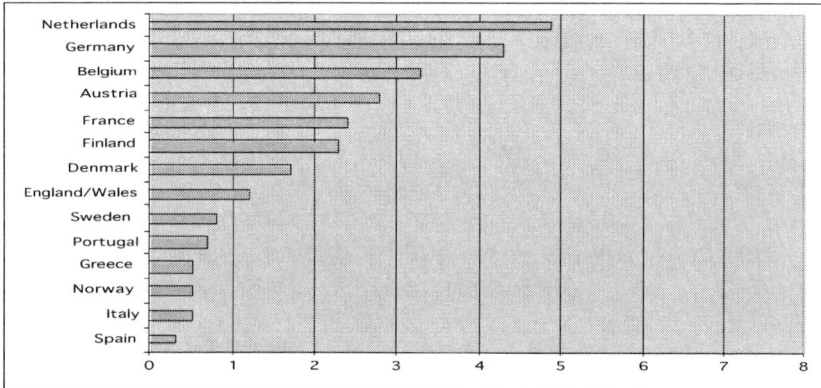

It is hard to say why the deinstitutionalisation movement started; probably there were many reasons – and not necessarily the same from sector to sector and country to country. The public purse probably had a larger impact in the field of psychiatry than in child protection, the image of inmates was clearly affected by the fact that some were war "heroes", the pharmacological revolution played a role, etc. One obvious background was, however, the severe criticisms of institutions, many of them summarised in Goffmans (1961) book Asylums:

– The labelling critique suggests that the treatment of certain groups actually makes their problem worse. Prison is a crime school. Institutions for intellectually disabled people are a less stimulating environment and it is likely that people learn less. The institutions are intellectually disabling. A diagnosis does not necessarily lead to productive treatment, but placement that deepens the problems. Custodial institutions are one example of such problem-producing placement.

- All need support in the environment for their self-image, feeling of self, identity etc. We tend to use markers such as hair-cut, clothes, friends, etc. to produce and support ourselves. When placed in dormitories with a lot of people with a similar haircut, same clothes, same furniture, same food, same rhythm of day – one is deprived of the needed environmental support for self – identity and potential devastating social-psychological effects.

- Institutions were gradually criticised for providing deplorable living conditions. Even though such scandals also occurred before the second world war, their number and impact increased during the 1960s – in a society that has the ambition of a welfare state. The question of justice and decent living conditions came to be important.

- Finally, a society claiming to be equalitarian, democratic and provide equal opportunities cannot on purpose place a group of citizens somewhere that is obviously negatively valued, stigmatised and even with an aura of danger.

In the coming deinstitutionalisation movement, children were first. In Norway, the ideology with respect to children changed rapidly during the 1960s. One started out with the idea that one needed expertise, special units and more special services in a white paper from 1964, but in three years (White Paper from 1967) this was changed to the idea that no special unit can provide a better care than the mother (a change that of course was supported by the fact that mom was cheaper).

During these years a new division of labour between the families and the public developed. Earlier it tended to be either-or, either the family had to cope with next to no help, or the child could be admitted to an institution which meant that the institutions took over more or less completely. The new division of labour was built on the principle that children live and grow up in their family, but also that it is a public responsibility to provide services that make it possible for both the child and the family to live a normal life. This implied day services (preschools, schools), respite care, economic support, technical aids, etc. This "normalisation" into family life was actually the first

85

"normalisation" and the fact that we no longer think of it as normalisation suggests its success – it has come to be taken for granted.

International research in brief

There is an enormous amount of research on deinstitutionalisation, the moving out of residential institutions, special schools and so on and it is of course not possible to pay justice to the variation in approaches, findings etc. The only reason I dare to raise this issue briefly is that it seems to be possible to point out a couple of very general aspects.

It would appear to be possible to group a large portion of this research into two distinct approaches. One is instrumental and sees integration as a means to some other goal – the effects research. Institutions were criticised for being a place where disabled children learned less, where there was more behaviour that was maladaptive than outside institutions. The logical follow-up question is thus: do they learn more after moving to mainstream settings? Since there are huge differences between disabled children, institutions and mainstream services, it is no surprise that findings vary. However, some meta-analyses suggest that (1) intellectually disabled people appear to learn more after relocation but maladaptive behaviour does not decrease, and (2) it is hard to find any systematic differences between special and mainstream schooling.[1]

These results, and particularly with respect to schools, have been interpreted extremely differently. Proponents of special schools tend to say that that is what they thought – there was no reason for this large and troublesome experiment, causing so many frustrations. Opponents of special schools on the other hand argue that if research cannot show that one type of school is clearly better than the other with respect to outcomes such as those related to learning, it all boils down to a question of values. From that perspective, inclusion is clearly to be preferred.

---

1. The instrumental "effects research" does not only address learning, adaptive and maladaptive behaviour but also issues like self-image, friendships etc. – but the "learning" side is definitely dominating.

This last interpretation also bridges over to the other main research approach. This one links up more directly to political values. It is taken for granted that inclusion, a society for all and full participation are important human and cultural values. The question is thus: Are such values really fulfilled – are the new services according to these values or are exclusion, segregation and stigmatisation reproduced in a new outfit? And also – are the living conditions better? Thus, the first approach relates to the criticism of the first bullet point on page 90, whereas the other approach is according to the third and fourth bullet points.

The rough answer is almost self-evident: most countries have moved along this road, but much is left to be done. There is a lot of reproduction of old problems in the new settings and the implementation has rarely been wholehearted. The ideal-reality gap has grown wide.

This ideal-reality approach also links on to the concepts or the understanding of both disability and integration. Integration is sometimes used as a term to indicate that disabled people are moved from a special to a regular setting. But as for the new understanding of disability, the real issue is about changing the school so that all children can be included. If one just moves disabled people to a regular school, without changing anything else, one cannot be surprised if problems are created. Thus, inclusion must mean the making of a new inclusive school. And this is one of the reasons why many want to replace the concept of integration with inclusion – to stress the fact that the bottom line of the programme is environmental change, relocating persons is just a small part of it.

Norwegian experiences

I present the Norwegian experiences, not just because that is my home country and thus the one I know best. It is also because it is one of the countries that has gone further down the road of integration than most, and as such, the experiences are of general interest – as a case. My presentation is based on a number of data sources, but mainly on a longitudinal project following disabled children born 1993-95 through childhood and adolescence (a survey N=625, interviews N=3, observations in preschools and schools: two data points; 1998/99 and 2002/3) and a study of children with learning difficulties in primary school (age 6-15) in the academic year 2000/01.

Preschool

At least from the beginning of the 1970s there was widespread agreement about the particular importance of nursery schools for disabled children. It was expected to facilitate socialising with non-disabled children, make it possible to grow up with the family and be an ideal place for stimulation and therapeutic interventions. Hence, since 1975 disabled children have had priority to nursery schools and in practice all disabled children who wanted it have been admitted since the mid-1980s. Few have to wait for more than a couple of months after filing the application, and actually more parents appear to feel that it is mandatory (because some local authorities make admittance to a nursery school an informal prerequisite for having special education, this is, however, not in keeping with Norwegian law).

Most disabled children go to regular units in regular preschools (83%). About 6% are in special preschools and another 6% in special units at regular preschools. The remaining are with their mother. Placement policy is partly related to the type of impairment. It is mostly children with multiple disabilities that continue to be segregated. However, segregation is also strongly related to the size of the municipality. Most small municipalities include all children, whereas the larger ones do not (cf. also next section on schools).

Real inclusion must also be social in the sense that spontaneous interaction with non-disabled children takes place. Does this occur? Yes and no. Disabled children do typically take part in all activities going on at the preschools and active rejection from other children is rare. Actually, rejection seems to take place the other way around more often, not intentionally, but because some disabled children give responses to other children's initiatives which are interpreted as "not interested". But on the other hand one can also observe frequent breakdowns in interaction. This is however rarely because of rejection but rather widespread interaction dynamics. Children move a lot, and that causes problems for children unable to walk or run. And if you do not understand the rules of a game (for instance because of intellectual disabilities), you are not exactly first choice to join that game. The main message is however what many parents stress: Disabled children do to a large extent take part, but often in "their own special way".

The main non-inclusive element appears to be the special education. Special educators tend to take children out of the group to practice face-to-face teaching with one child. The more important task of inclusion and co-operation with other children is left to unqualified assistants. This is however not the main reason why many parents are dissatisfied with special education. They tend to focus on shortage of resources and lack of organisation, particularly that you become so dependent on individuals – and if they get pregnant or change job, there is immediate risk of breakdown.

But in general, the preschool is the success story of inclusion policy, and parents express strong support and great satisfaction (this goes for both parents of children in regular and special settings).

School

The experiences from school are more mixed. In Norway all children have the right to education for 13-14 years, and it is compulsory for 10 years. No children have been regarded as uneducable since the middle of the 1970s. There is also an individual right to special education if a child cannot benefit from the regular curriculum. There have been conflicts between parents and municipalities on the quantity of special education, and a lot of parents file appeals. But all children have the same amount of hours at school as their peers, and most can also attend an after-school service.

Among disabled children, a large majority is included in regular schools. There are two main exceptions; children with hearing impairments and children with multiple/intellectual disabilities. For the first group, this is wanted by the Association of deaf people, because it is seen as the only way to provide a sign language setting. As for children with multiple or intellectual disabilities, the parents' society is strongly in favour of inclusion. The special school system for this group has been dismantled; however, practice among local authorities (responsible for the education) is to reproduce segregating arrangements for some. The new outfit of segregation is, however, less spectacular than earlier. The typical form of segregation is special classes at regular schools, sometimes at clustered schools, but even segregated special schools do exist.

This does not mean that all intellectually disabled children benefit from special arrangements. A large portion is at regular schools, but it is so linked to age that it is close to meaningless to give one figure to indicate proportions. In Figure 4 the percentage of intellectually disabled children not in regular classes by age is presented. The number in regular classes drops from 81% in preschools via 56 in the first 3-4 schools years to 7% after the tenth year at school. The practice of segregation is also partly linked to how disabled the child is, but equally strong to the size of the municipality. Segregation is much more common in larger municipalities and densely populated areas.

Figure 4: Percentage of intellectually disabled children in regular/not regular classes by age/grade. Source:

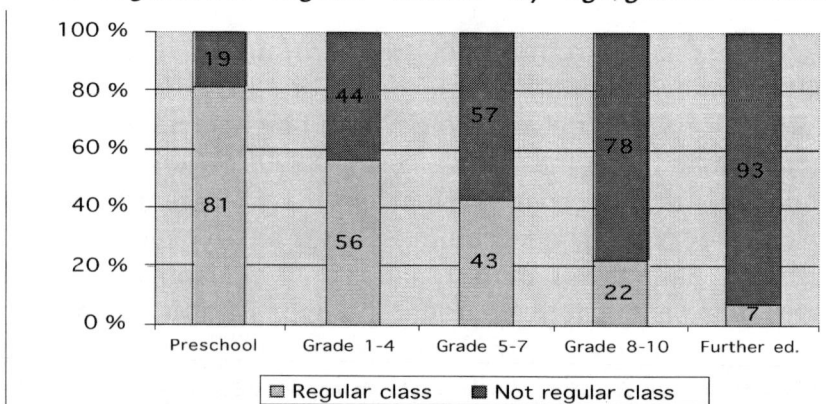

The experiences of disabled children at school tend to be less favourable than at preschool, according to our observational studies. Although I cannot spend time on details now, the ability to handle diversity and disability, and in particular intellectual disability, appears in school to lag far behind preschools.

However, analyses of parents' opinions and experiences do not give much support to the idea that segregation is better. Some argue that at a regular school an intellectually disabled child will be isolated and lonely, meet staff with poorer qualifications, and be more vulnerable to staff turnover. According to our data there are few differences with respect to loneliness and staff qualifications, maybe some more bullying but also much more positive interaction with non-disabled children at regular schools (statistically controlled for severity of disability).

As in preschool, special education does for a large part tend to take place outside the regular classroom. This goes for all types of special education, whether it is a small or large portion of one's curriculum. One-to-one teaching outside the regular classroom appears almost as the emblem of modern special education. The consequence of this is that neither regular nor special education need to change teaching practices much – thus the one-to-one teaching appears almost like the perfect defence of professional traditions among teachers.

This does not mean that inclusion at school is a failure, but it is more difficult or challenging than in preschools. There are very few indications of benefits of segregation, but there are a substantial number of issues that need to be solved better than today – including issues related to the wholehearted implementation of the current political ideals.

Family life

According to the new division of labour between families and the public, children are expected to grow up at home with day services and other types of support. The policy is to facilitate a normal family life and a normal childhood. This can imply a number of things, but at least some basic life structures such as divorce/separation of families, labour market participation and experiences with the public service agencies are relevant to the "evaluation" of the state of affairs.

As for marriage and divorce, the following appears to be the case. When children are small (3-5 years) the main difference seems to be that parents who live together as partners more often marry if a child is disabled. Fewer cohabit without being married. In middle childhood (8-10 years of age) fewer families appear to have experienced a separation. 20% compared to 28% of non-disabled children at this age live with only one of their biological parents. Thus, through middle childhood, a disabled child appears to protect against separation – but of course for different reasons among which some may be felt less than voluntary. It is nevertheless contrary to typical prejudices. We have no reliable data for children older than 10 years.

As for siblings, small disabled children tend to have as many siblings as other children at the same age. This is logical since few families have had the time to produce more children yet. When children are 8-10 years of age, families with disabled children tend to have fewer children than other families (20% of disabled compared to 10% among all children at the same age have no sibling). Nevertheless, 46% of the disabled 8 to 10-year-olds do have a younger sibling. Thus, the difference to other families is small.

As for labour market participation, fathers are very similar to other fathers, but some have changed job in order to avoid travelling, shift work etc. Mothers do work less frequently than other mothers (difference 8%), and if working, they work fewer hours (% part time work increasing from 7% difference at child age 3-5, to 19%-difference at child age 8-10).

In short – the families appear more similar than expected to other families, but gradually the labour market participation of mothers falls behind. We should also be aware of the fact that differences are likely to be more significant with respect to social life, leisure activities etc.

92

The big challenge faced by those with a disabled child in contemporary Norway is, however, the relation to the service system. Families are in general satisfied with the services, but at the same time very critical. They tend to be supportive and satisfied with the services themselves, but critical to (1) the co-ordination, and in particular (2) the access. Parents do have to spend such a lot of time co-ordinating services that it is described as an additional parental role – the role as service administrator. The most important point is the access, the fight with service agencies to get access to services, the appeals and complaints, etc. It appears that the protection of the public purse against people who are not eligible for a service also creates barriers to people who are eligible – barriers that actually become part of everyday life of parents of disabled children.

Thus, the new division of labour works in some respects. Family life is in basic structures not very different from other families, and people receive services of a reasonable quality. Family life is close to the typical even though there is substantially more childcare. In other respects the division of labour does not work, and this in particular applies to the intersection between family and the public – where the access to services is at stake. The lack of information, first-hand refusals, appeals, waiting, fighting and quarrelling appears or is experienced as totally unnecessary and an undue burden on parents.

Concluding remarks

Even though many aspects of the deinstitutionalisation have been a relative success, we are confronted with some major challenges that need to be addressed. As for the case of children, I will as a conclusion point out three challenges:

- Access: The threshold to services, established to avoid misuse produces an undue extra burden on parents and also unequal treatment of families.

- Inclusion: There is a need to work with school practices, teaching methods and child grouping in order to make the school more inclusive. A programme for school development is needed.

- Special education: There is a need for a renewal of special education practices and methods. It is a challenge to change it from counteracting to supporting current inclusion policy.

From Institutions to Inclusion

Ms Diana HOOVER
Executive Director
Mental Disability Advocacy Centre (MDAC)
Budapest, Hungary

Abstract

Over 1 million children, disabled and elderly live in institutions in Central and Eastern Europe (CEE) and Central Asia (CAR). Though institutions were considered "best practice" treatment for disabled (and orphaned) during communism, numbers of institutionalised have in fact increased post-transition. This increase has been fostered by economic upheavals as well as by chaotic health system transition, from socialised to privatised systems. Families without the wherewithal to provide for vulnerable family members have increasingly abandoned their needy to institutions. Demographics in CEE and CAR show increases in population average age, together with falling birth rates in these regions, pointing to the potential for even greater rates of institutionalisation in coming years.

It is now widely accepted that community-based treatment is the best practice for most people with disabilities. This fact is enshrined in international human rights treaties (such as the Convention on the Rights of the Child) and in principles and recommendations at UN and European levels (MI Principles, Standard Rules, Council of Europe Recommendations). Further, institutional environments have been shown to be damaging to the emotional and physical development of children (Bowlby) and to support inhuman and degrading treatment of people within their bounds.

In CEE and CAR, most institutions are little more than warehouses, often operating on less than $1 per inmate per day, providing no rehabilitation and no means of ever transitioning out. Moreover, many institutions in these regions have higher than average mortality rates (with inmates dying from malnutrition over long periods of time and hypothermia) as well as overuse of medications and abuse of restraints (such as cage beds).

Justifications for deinstitutionalisation are clear. The path toward deinstitutionalisation is less clear. Obstacles include resistance from institutions and psychiatrists (who too often still receive funding by filling beds), widespread stigma against people with disabilities (at political, professional, community and family levels), lack of functioning models of community-based (CB) treatment, lack of staff trained in rehabilitative care or CB care, lack of legislative frameworks allowing restructuring and financing of CB mental health and social service systems, etc.

A diversity of approaches to overcoming these obstacles is needed. Piloting best practice community-based models is one approach (used in Slovenia, Kosovo, Lithuania among other countries); providing information about abuses in institutional systems to governments and media is another approach; directly challenging human rights abuses within institutional environments via litigation to prompt changes in legislation and practice is yet another approach.

MDAC focuses on legal advocacy: litigation and law reform via national and international channels, based on solid research. MDAC's flagship work thus far on cage bed use in CEE has prompted bans in Hungary and initiated dialogue about cage bed use in the Czech Republic and Slovakia. MDAC is now initiating research into human rights abuses within guardianship systems in CEE and CAR systems which currently allow many people to be detained and treated

95

against their will. Analysis in light of international best practices and human rights standards (including the Council of Europe Recommendation No. R(99)4) will follow, as a baseline for advocacy at governmental and inter-governmental levels. This presentation will detail these issues.

Presentation

Good afternoon! My name is Diana Hoover and I am the Executive Director of the Mental Disability Advocacy Center, based in Budapest. MDAC, for those of you who don't know us, is an international legal advocacy NGO. Our focus is litigation and law reform to protect and promote the rights of people with mental health problems and people with intellectual disabilities. I think I can say that we are the only NGO in Europe thus far focused on strategic litigation at national and international levels for this target group.

As a sort of real life illustration of this morning's presentations about the use of UN and European human rights frameworks, I will spend the next 20 minutes explaining the path that MDAC has taken to uphold the rights of people with mental disabilities in Central and Eastern Europe, our target region.

Though it is clear that institutions in and of themselves create environments where abuse of human rights is easier than in community-based services, as you heard from my colleague, Professor Tøssebro, there are numerous challenges in reaching the goal of deinstitutionalisation and best practice, least restrictive, alternatives.

In CEE and Central Asia, the barriers are stark: Large isolated institutions are the norm, left over from the Soviet period, a medicalized view of disability is evident in the profession entitled "defectology". Legislative and financial frameworks (when they exist) still favour institutions. Most inmates of institutions are warehoused for life with little rehabilitation available and no community-based alternatives. The physical conditions of institutions are so poor that mortality rates from malnutrition and hypothermia (where known) are shocking. And institutions are breeding grounds for dehumanization, allowing inhuman and degrading treatment (such as placing inmates in cage beds) to take place far from public scrutiny.

Nearly 15 years after the barriers between East and West Europe have dissolved and several years after a number of new member states have acceded to the EU, most people with mental disabilities in CEE and CAR remain behind walls, in poorly monitored confinement, subject to human rights abuses and early death.

This is not to say that efforts have not been made. There are numerous pilot projects across the region beginning to show that alternative community-based treatment is possible (some financed by the World Bank; many started by local and international NGOs). Reports about institutional conditions have been publicised broadly by independent groups such as Amnesty International or Inclusion Europe and by intergovernmental bodies such as the Council of Europe's own Convention for the Prevention of Torture.

Media has taken up the call for anti-stigmatization campaigns (referencing recent BBC World News and Radio 4 programmes on cage beds).

And WHO and other agencies have worked with governments to revamp mental health legislation and financing and to initiate improved professional training programmes.

Change is beginning. However, troubling to a legal advocacy NGO such as MDAC is the continued lack of any form of patients' rights (including support for user-led efforts), lack of local independent monitoring systems and lack of sufficient national legal protection to guard against abuse and to provide avenues for challenging institutionalisation as a whole. Strategic cases, such as the 1999 Olmstead case in the US which affirmed the right of people with mental disabilities to least restrictive forms of care and created deinstitutionalisation guidelines prescribed in law, have not been litigated in CEE/CAR. Not enough challenges have been brought before legal bodies and precedents are few and far between. There are few lawyers interested in mental disability issues and access to justice is near impossible for those institutionalised (and too often stripped of legal personality through guardianship).

To address this gap, MDAC has worked with national lawyers to bring 18 cases thus far to national courts and to the European Court of Human Rights. We have also held trainings, in partnership with the Council of Europe in countries of the region for lawyers, NGOs and disability activists, and just a couple of weeks ago, had our first annual Council of Europe sponsored training for mental disability litigators from CEE here at the European Court of Human Rights in Strasbourg.

Of course, legal advocacy encompasses more than litigation: winning a case is not winning the battle. Solid baseline information is crucial to show that an individual case is not just a fluke in the system but the tip of the iceberg of systemic abuses. And, follow-up advocacy at national and inter-governmental levels is necessary for systemic changes.

MDAC approaches legal advocacy by initiating research into neglected human rights concerns. I will give you a brief overview of two issues we are working on as an example. The first is cage beds.

MDAC started by visiting more than 20 wards in social care homes and psychiatric hospitals in 4 EU accession countries (Hungary, Czech Republic, Slovakia and Slovenia). We interviewed hundreds of key informants including users, mental health professionals, service providers and government officials. Through this research, we found that cage beds were routinely used to physically detain people with dementia, psychiatric illness, or severe intellectual disabilities sometimes for months or years, that the beds were/are often used as a substitute for staff, and as a form of punishment. People who had experienced a cage bed routinely described it as a degrading and damaging experience.

In 2003, we launched a report in the European Parliament. In 2004, we brought a case to national level courts of a man who had died locked in a cage bed during a fire. We had ministry meetings, we launched press releases. In June 2004, the

Minister of Health banned cage beds. However, the struggle continues. In early 2005 we will publish a follow-up report on steps taken since 2003 and next steps needed.

We have just launched a new multi-year project on abuses within guardianship systems in CEE. Guardianship was intended to protect those who lacked capacity to protect themselves and needed a surrogate to make decisions. However, anecdotal evidence has revealed that this system often perpetuates human rights abuses by removing legal personality from someone who has capacity. This occurs because there is no functioning system of judicial review of capacity or subsequent guardianship appointment in CEE. Much worse, those placed under guardianship often end up in institutions and institutional directors are often named as guardians creating a situation in which no legal appeal can be made by individuals suffering abuses in institutions.

This project will start by comparing national guardianship legislation in 5 CEE countries to international best practice and human rights standards (such as the Council of Europe Recommendation No. R(99)4), will proceed with looking at guardianship practices in these countries and will produce a report to be used in advocacy efforts (including legislative reform and litigation) at a later stage.

I will just conclude by saying that there are many ways to promote deinstitutionalisation. Legal advocacy is only one route, but it is a necessary component. Without services prescribed and supported by law, including human rights treaties, people with mental disabilities are at risk of remaining marginalised. I will end with this quote from Mr. Alvaro Gil-Robles, Council of Europe Commissioner for Human Rights:

"The dehumanisation of persons with mental disabilities and the subsequent loss of their status as subjects of human rights is to be countered at every turn and with all available means."

99

Challenging Human Rights Violations of People with Disabilities

Ms Bardhylka KOSPIRI
Advocacy Group Coordinator
Albanian Disability Rights Foundation
Tirana

Abstract

We live in a disabling society. The European Action Plan on Equal Opportunities for people with disabilities presents a plan for changing this. Disability is not something individuals have, what they have are impairments. These impairments may be physical, sensory, neurological, psychiatric, intellectual or of other nature.

Disability is the process which happens when one group of people creates barriers by designing a world only for themselves, not taking into account the impairments other people have. The Albanian society – as others - is built in a way that assumes that everybody can move quickly over the road and that everybody can see all signs, read directions, hear announcements, reach buttons, has the strength to open heavy doors and has stable moods and perceptions.

Disability relates to the interaction between the person with the impairment and the environment. People and groups of people should not be judged by one particular aspect of their lives – whether it's their race, gender, age or impairment. Individual beliefs and assumptions, as well as the practices of institutions, mean that many disabled people are not able to access things that many non-disabled people take for granted.

The desire to break down the barriers that cause disability is also closely linked to ideas about the human rights of people with impairments. Without human rights nobody can live as a full human being. Disabled people are entitled to the same human rights as all other citizens. The first article of the Universal Declaration on Human Rights states: "All human beings are free and equal in dignity and rights".

100

In order to achieve this goal, all communities should celebrate the diversity within their communities and seek to ensure that disabled people can enjoy the full range of human rights: civil, political, social, economical and cultural as acknowledged by different Conventions, the European Social Charter (revised), different EU Treaties, and in the different national constitutions.

Fundamental rights contained in the European Convention for the Protection of Human Rights and Fundamental Freedoms, its Protocols and the European Social Charter such as the right to education, the right to work, the right to private and family life, the right to protection of health and social security, the right to protection against poverty and social exclusion, the right to adequate housing etc. are still inaccessible to many people with disabilities who, according to WHO, represent 10% of the population. People with disabilities, and to a higher degree those in eastern European countries, experience human rights violations in their everyday life.

The reforms to create market economies in the countries of central and eastern Europe have created new possibilities for citizens. But often disabled people have been excluded from this process and marginalised from the economic benefits available, so that their economic conditions are often harder then before and they have to fight for their survival. The transitory period from the communist regime to a democracy is characterised by deterioration of social, economic and other aspects of life in countries in transition, including Albania. Although more than ten years have already passed since the fall of the communist regime, Albania is still facing serious difficulties related to the socio-economic development.

Based on a survey carried out by the Albanian Disability Rights Foundation (ADRF), in different regions in Albania, 25% of the interviewed people are affected by disability and a higher proportion of those living in chronic poverty (based again on a survey done by ADRF almost 60% live below the poverty level). The basic cause of poverty for people with disabilities is exclusion; exclusion from social economic and

101

political life, exclusion that leads to lack of resources lower expectations, poor health and poor education. So people with disabilities experience chronic poverty in terms of income, as well as wider exclusion. Excluded from mainstream social, economic and political opportunities, meaning lack of exercise of human rights throughout their lives, disabled people frequently fall further and further in chronic poverty and have little possibility to come out of this cycle.

Disabled children are at a huge disadvantage as they grow up having been excluded from formal and informal education. This has an impact not only on qualifications and experience but also on levels of confidence and self-esteem. As a result later in life, they have restricted employment opportunities, due to discrimination, lack of education, experience and confidence.

Albania has started the process of joining the EU. Being an eastern European potential candidate for EU, it has a long way ahead and a lot of responsibilities to take. Among the basic principles that are core to the agreement for the stabilization and association process are those of in respect of human rights. All people should enjoy the basic human rights, irrespective of sex, religion, nationality or disability.

ADRF is striving throughout its activities to ensure that respect for human rights exists on an equal basis for everybody in a democratic society, especially for people with disabilities who are facing discrimination in all areas of life. All sectors, private and public, are insufficient in providing services both in quantity and quality, so people with disabilities, considered as belonging to the population at risk, or amongst the most vulnerable groups in the society, are suffering the consequences of service insufficiency. They are deprived of health and social care, employment and freedom of movement, education, personal integrity and social security etc. The government seems to be trying to address the problems facing the country and people in a positive responsible way. Civil society in fact is so far considered to be a driving force to real change; it has grown and developed and many signs of partnership between civil society organisations and government organisations are present.

The respect of human rights, fundamental freedoms and dignity of people with disabilities is a responsibility of a society as a whole, but also of each individual member.

Presentation

We live in a disabling society. The European Action Plan on Equal Opportunities for people with disabilities presents a plan for changing this.

Disability is not something individuals have, what they have are impairments. These impairments may be physical, sensory, neurological, psychiatric, intellectual or of other nature.

Disability is the process which happens when one group of people creates barriers by designing a world only for themselves, not taking into account the impairments other people have. The Albanian society – as others - is built in a way that assumes that everybody can move quickly over the road and that everybody can see all signs, read directions, hear announcements, reach buttons, has the strength to open heavy doors and has stable moods and perceptions.

Disability relates to the interaction between the person with the impairment and the environment. People and groups of people should not be judged by one particular aspect of their lives – whether it's their race, gender, age or impairment. Individual beliefs and assumptions, as well as the practices of institutions, mean that many disabled people are not able to access things that many non-disabled people take for granted.

The desire to break down the barriers that cause disability is also closely linked to ideas about the human rights of people with impairments. Without human rights nobody can live as a full human being. Disabled people are entitled to the same human rights as all other citizens. The first article of the Universal Declaration on Human Rights states: "All human beings are free and equal in dignity and rights".

103

In order to achieve this goal, all communities should celebrate the diversity within their communities and seek to ensure that disabled people can enjoy the full range of human rights: civil, political, social, economical and cultural as acknowledged by the different Conventions, European Social Charter (revised) different EU Treaties and in the different national constitutions.

Fundamental rights contained in the European Convention for the Protection of Human Rights and Fundamental Freedoms, its Protocols and in the European Social Charter, such as the right to education, the right to work, the right to private and family life, the right to protection of health and social security, the right to protection against poverty and social exclusion, the right to adequate housing etc. are still inaccessible to many people with disabilities.

People with disabilities, who, based on statistics, represent 10% of the population, experience human rights violations in their everyday life. This inequality is more apparent in eastern European countries.

The reforms to create market economies in the countries of central and eastern Europe have created new possibilities for citizens. But often disabled people have been excluded from this process and marginalised from the economic benefits available, so that their economic conditions are often harder then before and they have to fight for their survival. The transitory period from the communist regime to a democracy is characterised by deterioration of social, economic and other aspects of life in Albania. Although more than ten years have already passed since the fall of communist regime, Albania is still facing serious difficulties related to its socio-economic development.

Based on a survey carried out by the Albanian Disability Rights Foundation (ADRF), in different regions in Albania, 25% of the interviewed people are affected by disability and a higher proportion of those living in chronic poverty (based again on a survey completed by ADRF almost 60% live below the poverty level). The basic cause of poverty for people with disabilities is exclusion, exclusion from social economic and

104

political life, exclusion that leads to lack of resources lower expectations, poor health and poor education. So people with disabilities experience chronic poverty in terms of income, as well as wider exclusion. Excluded from mainstream social, economic and political opportunities, meaning lack of exercise of human rights throughout their lives, disabled people frequently fall further and further into chronic poverty and have little possibility to come out of this cycle.

Disabled children are at a huge disadvantage as they grow up having been excluded from formal and informal education. This has an impact not only on qualifications and experience but also on levels of confidence and self-esteem. As a result later in life, they have restricted employment opportunities, due to discrimination, lack of education, experience and confidence. Attempts and interventions to support and help children with disabilities have been and are numerous, and at the same time achievements as well as failures have been notified.

Treatment of humiliation and charity, predominant until the 1960s or 1970s in different countries in the world, were replaced in later years by practices of treatment in special settings, treatment in special schools or special institutions for children with disabilities. The main arguments that have supported these practices are related to the reasoning that the work is better organised in small homogenous groups, that they have the proper conditions to treat children properly etc. On the other hand these institutions have been critised for artificial conditions and isolation; for not preparing children with disabilities to adequately face real life; lack of positive models; decline in the requirements from the staff due to adaptation, stigmatisation etc.

Facing the continuous controversies and following campaigns to respect the rights of children with disabilities, a number of special institutions have been closed. However, a good number of institutions have been renovated. It is a fact that in many industrialised countries due to the number of problems these children face, and, in particular, for children with profound

105

multiple disabilities, special institutions are still deemed as being valuable and necessary. Despite these developments, there still remains a necessity for these institutions to be improved, without undermining the combination of alternatives or new opportunities or options that might arise.

In our country, though at a later stage, education and care in specialised centres or schools was the main way in which people with disabilities were treated.

The beginning of the institutionalised treatment of the children with disabilities was in the 1960s. The first attempts were related to the first classes opened for blind and deaf children. The work gradually led to the establishment of the National Institute in Tirana, which later split in two institutions, one for deaf people and one for blind people.

The Ministry of Health established for children with development problems, mental retardation etc. some residential centres. In the last years, these centres have been placed under the responsibility of the Ministry of Labour and Social Protection.

After the 1970s, and in order to deal with the large number of cases of children with disabilities leaving school and in order to meet the requirement of compulsory education, it was deemed important to establish special schools for children with disabilities. Special curricula were prepared for the education of the children with disabilities in these special schools.

In Albania, there are currently 10 special schools, 5 residential centres, 2 day-care centres, (mainly for persons with mental retardation or learning disabilities) and two national institutions: one for blind people one for deaf people. While the last two serve the needs of all the country the other institutions struggle to meet 3% of the demand. There is a lot to be done with respect to the efficiency and the work of these institutions. The level of staff expertise is gained through short-term training or passed from generation to generation, staff do not tend to follow proper training programmes. Due to the variety of cases and problems encountered, these institutions often lack a clear profile which has inevitably influenced the quality of their work. As for the institutional arrangements, neither the Ministry of Education nor the Science and Ministry of Labour and Social Protection had the proper structures. Thus, without undermining the values of the above ministries, there has not been any proper special education system with regard to the organisation, management and proper functioning .

In addition to the work carried out by the above institutions, it is important to mention the initiatives of different NGOs to create centres or set up support services such as training or development centres etc.

Today, the small number of centres and schools that exist are considered a privilege of some cities. In a considerable number of towns, in particular in rural areas (where 60% of the population live), no institutions of special education exist. The data of empirical studies carried out lately shows that 2.7% up to 3.2% of children of school age show slight problems (mental retardation, emotional disorders, physical or sensorial disabilities etc.). From 500,000 pupils that attend primary school, 10-13% show signs of different learning disabilities (in speaking, reading, writing, maths etc.).

The findings of the surveys show that for severe cases, in general, parents want their children to be treated in special institutions. Looking for solutions families move to other cities or immigrate, while most of the children with disabilities are kept inside and are forced to live in isolation away from society and structures of social life with a lack of services or proper care.

Parents of children with slight or moderate disabilities, which represent the biggest number, try to include their children in regular schools together with their peers. The present laws neither forbid nor guarantee this. In facing the school reality, parents have different experiences that vary from declared rejection to silent acceptance. Thanks to the pressure exercised from parents a part of these pupils manage to attend regular schools. But after one to two years they leave the school, as they cannot survive there. The medical model of disability seems still to be strong.

The data of the 1998 study organised by the Albanian Disability Rights Foundation "National Opinion Survey" on public attitudes of the Albanians towards people with disabilities shows that 83.3% of the Albanian public thinks that this social group is neglected and that little attention is paid to them. 43.9% of the interviewed think that the economic situation has been a problem for their integration, 28.8% believe that it is due to the political system and 34.2% think that it has to do with the mentality and culture in Albania. With regard to human rights and the tolerance of society towards these people, 81.6% of the interviewed think that they have the same right to education and work as everyone else.

In general, the data of the survey shows a chaotic situation in this field, but at the same time it stresses the need to increase public awareness for changes needed and promotion of new approaches as part of the democratisation of the Albanian society.

Despite difficult conditions, including a large number of pupils per class, schools teachers have managed over the past few years to encourage and keep pupils with disabilities attending their classes. In this respect a number of successful cases can be mentioned. However, despite the willingness and commitment of these teachers we should admit that their actions have not brought about changes to the practices and work methods used in classes, and they have not contributed to the restructuring of the school in general.

The first attempts towards integration practices in Albania date back to 1990. During the last decade, along with the democratic changes, and other reasons, it can be said that more and more parents refuse to accept that their children attend special institutions. They have been conscious of the possibilities for their children and have increased their demands and expectations for acceptance and education of children with disabilities in regular schools considering it not a privilege but a right that everyone should have.

During the last seven years the inclusion of children with disabilities in mainstream education in Albania has become a process that has been promoted mainly by civil society. However, government policies and practices in this respect have been very scarce due to lack of resources, old mentalities and, moreover, lack of good will. Yet, after effective joint lobbying and advocacy of disability NGOs, mainly centred around ADRF, the Ministry of Education and Science (MES) embraced the concept of inclusive education in September 2002 and produced a set of regulations, formally known as the Normative Dispositions of Public Education. In 2004 the Albanian government produced the first draft of the Strategy for Persons with Disabilities in which inclusive education for children with disabilities is given a substantial place. Inclusive education is also mainstreamed in the overall Strategy of Education compiled by the MES. So this is just the beginning of a process which requires substantial practical intervention.

The basic principles accompanying the whole process should be:

– The right to education for all disabled children as the first key issue.
– Inclusive education can only be a success if the adequate support is provided to the child. Inclusion without support is deemed to be a failure.
– There has to be a choice, but for choice to be real, there must be real options.
– Special education should never be an excuse for not making mainstream education accessible to disabled children.

If we manage to compile a complete framework of policies to realize inclusion, if we enable their implementation, if we raise public awareness regarding the essential importance of equality and full participation, then the negative image of disability will no longer prevail. Disability will become an issue belonging to the whole society and there will be no need to appeal to "design and provide services for us too", instead there would be an emphasis on the comparative evaluation of the service for all citizens where needs of every citizen including people with disabilities are met.

WORKSHOP 2
DISABLED CHILDREN AND THEIR FAMILIES

Chair: Mr Helmut HEINEN, Belgium

The Council of Europe's Revised Strategy for Social Cohesion in relation to the integration of children with disabilities

Ms Marie-Cécile VADEAU-DUCHER
Chairperson of the European Committee for
Social Cohesion (CDCS)
Ministry of Health, the Family and Persons with Disabilities
France

Abstract

Human rights have been the Council of Europe's main concern for nearly 60 years. And promoting human rights also means promoting the social rights enshrined in the European Social Charter.

With its 46 member states, the Council of Europe can now be said to cover almost the whole of Europe. It has a duty to play a particularly active role in promoting social cohesion and combating poverty and financial insecurity throughout our continent.

At the second Summit of Heads of State and Government in 1997, social cohesion was defined as "one of the foremost needs of the wider Europe ... and an essential complement to the promotion of human rights and dignity."

It is therefore important to underline that:

– social cohesion must be a priority for the Council of Europe,

– social cohesion must be based on human rights,

– social cohesion concerns us all and must be a shared responsibility.

When it was set up in 1998, the European Committee for Social Cohesion (CDCS) began by defining the framework for its activity and drawing up a statement of intent on social policies. This led in 2000 to the Strategy for Social Cohesion, followed in 2004 by the revised Strategy for Social Cohesion, setting out the priorities for action by governments and the Council of Europe in the social policy sector.

Particular attention has been paid to the rights and needs of vulnerable individuals and groups (women, children, people with disabilities, victims of human trafficking and marginalised groups). The CDCS' activities concerning children and families have not been specifically geared towards children with disabilities or their parents. However, some issues are more general and I believe it is important to stress that children with disabilities are, above all, children and parents of children with disabilities are, above all, parents.

The various activities may nevertheless provide inspiration for or, indeed, help other working groups focusing on the specific needs of people with disabilities.

It goes without saying that the CDCS takes account in its work of children's rights as enshrined in the texts of the Council of Europe (European Social Charter, recommendations of the Parliamentary Assembly of the Council of Europe) and the United Nations (United Nations Convention on the Rights of the Child), and the texts it draws up include the concept of respect for the human dignity of children.

Through the new Committee of Experts on Children and Families, the CDCS will be looking more closely in the next few years at the relations between parents and children. Given the fact that parents must now more than ever before help their children to find their way through the constraints of modern life, the aim will be to assist parents in this task of helping their children prepare their future in the best possible way.

112

Proposals will be made during the conference on establishing closer links between the committee responsible for children and families and its counterpart dealing with the rehabilitation and integration of people with disabilities.

Presentation

As Chairperson of the European Committee for Social Cohesion (CDCS) I would like to say how pleased I am to take part in this "disabled children and their families" workshop. I have been asked to speak to you about the revised social cohesion strategy prepared by the CDCS and to present it to you with a view to children with disabilities.

As you already know, human rights have been the main focus of the Council of Europe's action for almost 60 years. Human rights also include the social rights that are so important for the European Social Charter and the CDCS.

With its 46 member states, the Council of Europe now covers virtually all of geographical Europe. It therefore has the duty to play a specific and active role in promoting social cohesion and combating insecurity throughout the continent.

In 1997, at the Second Summit of Heads of State and Government, social cohesion was defined as "one of the foremost needs of the wider Europe and ... an essential complement to the promotion of human rights and dignity".

That is why it is important to point out that:

– social cohesion must be a priority for the Council of Europe,

– social cohesion must be founded on human rights,

– social cohesion concerns us all and must be a shared responsibility.

I will therefore present to you:

1. the European Committee for Social Cohesion (CDCS) and its strategy for social cohesion,

2. the CDCS' activities in the field of children and families and its work on child/ parent relationships,

113

3. future avenues for work that we could develop to help disabled children and their families.

The European Committee for Social Cohesion and its strategy for social cohesion

The European Committee for Social Cohesion, known as the CDCS, was set up in 1998 following the Second Summit of Heads of State and Government. Its terms of reference assign to it 4 major tasks in promoting social and economic progress in Council of Europe member states, i.e. to:

1. promote the social standards embodied in the European Social Charter and the Revised European Social Charter;

2. promote social cohesion in Europe through integrated multidisciplinary responses to social issues;

3. exchange information and good practice on issues relating to social cohesion;

4. finally, it is the CDCS' responsibility to execute and implement treaties such as the European Social Security Code.

The strategy for social cohesion

Since it was first established, the committee has committed itself to an important task: outlining the context for its activities and drafting its statement of intent: the strategy for social cohesion,[1] which presents the priority activities of governments and the Council of Europe in the field of social policies. This strategy was revised in 2004.[2] Its activities initially focused on:

– access to social rights: i.e. to social protection, housing and employment,

– urban social policies,

– the rights and protection of children,

– dependent senior citizens.

---

1. Adopted by the Committee of Ministers on 12 May 2000
2. Adopted by the Committee of Ministers on 31 March 2004

Special attention has been given to the rights and needs of vulnerable individuals and groups (women, children, families in difficult situations, for example single-parent families, people with disabilities, victims of trafficking in human beings and marginalised people). This commitment to these people and policies has been renewed and reinforced by the revised strategy for social cohesion – of which you will find copies in this meeting-room. For each of these groups, we have sought to highlight the importance of their well-being in the context of sustainable development and of future generations – young people and children – by adjusting policies to the specific needs of groups such as people with disabilities or the elderly, for example. This is the approach adopted by Mr Marc Maudinet in his report on "access to social rights for people with disabilities in Europe".

Finally, with regard to the Third Summit of Heads of State and Government, which will take place in Warsaw in May 2005, the CDCS wishes to continue its work on the future of social cohesion by setting up a group of wise people, which will have the task of studying the European social model at the beginning of the 21st century.

The CDCS' activities in the field of children and its discussions on child/parent relationships

Now that I have briefly described the strategy for social cohesion, I would like to turn to the subject which is of particular interest to you today in this workshop on "disabled children and their families" and describe the CDCS' activities in the field of children and families.

These activities did not specifically concern children with disabilities or their parents but a number of problems remain and it seems to me to be important to point out that children with disabilities are first and foremost children. They need to have contact with others, to play, to laugh, to communicate with others and to receive an education. And the parents of children with disabilities are above all parents with their joys and their sorrows, their cares, their stress, their life as a couple, and their working life - if their child's disability allows

115

them to hold down a job. Our work will, I hope, help these people.

But let me be quite clear that when I say "children with disabilities are first and foremost children and the parents of children with disabilities are above all parents" I do not mean to tar everyone with the same brush, if you will excuse the expression, and to deny that these people have to deal with many problems. We know that the main problem for children with disabilities is how they integrate and adjust to society, beginning with education and school, from kindergarten to secondary level, with the aid of social and medical institutions and services. There are also other problems such as the availability of special physical aids and access to new technologies.

The problems which parents usually encounter take on a completely different dimension and present much greater difficulties for the parents of children with disabilities, for example:

- the problem of reconciling working and family life;
- financial problems - in some member states financial assistance does not always meet children's needs in terms of health and equipment. One of the parents is also often obliged to give up their job to look after the child;
- health problems - psychological support may prove to be useful and sometimes necessary;
- last but not least, problems of stress.

First of all, however, I think we have to bear in mind the fact that it is not always easy to be a child and a parent, and that it is even less easy to be a child with a disability or the parent of a disabled child.

Our work has also taken account of the rights of children as set out:

- in the United Nations treaties and the United Nations Convention on the Rights of the Child;
- in Council of Europe texts: the European Convention on Human Rights, the European Social Charter and various recommendations on this subject;

– and the texts drawn up under the auspices of the CDCS, which include the concept of respect for the human dignity of the child.

In recent years, the CDCS has sought to extend its thinking on matters concerning children. Through its Forum for Children and Families – which was the relevant committee in this field until early 2004 – it focused its activities on:

– day care for children,

– the need to place children at risk in institutions,

– children, democracy and participation in society.

Recommendations have been made and the latest one concerns the need to place children at risk in institutions, for example in cases where keeping children in their families would place them at risk because their parents are alcoholics, drug-addicts, depressive, or beat their children. This recommendation gave rise to numerous, fruitful discussions and debates but the prime consideration was always the best interests of the child.

The Forum for Children and Families has also discussed issues such as:

– the need to have a European Ombudsperson for the Rights of Children

– psychological violence and the neglect of children

– the abolition of corporal punishment in European countries.

With regard to the last two points, it must be mentioned that children with disabilities are also victims of abuse and violence, as was shown by the Committee on the Rehabilitation and the Integration of People with disabilities (CD-P-RR) - the relevant Council of Europe committee in the field of disability – in one of its latest reports presented to the Conference of European Ministers in Malaga in 2003.

---

1. (1) "Protecting children against corporal punishment – awareness-raising campaigns ". (2)"Eliminating corporal punishment: a human rights imperative for Europe's children".

The CDCS, for its part, intends to shortly publish two reports on protecting children against corporal punishment.[1]

Child/parent relationships

In practice, the first experience of social cohesion is within families. The CDCS is aware of this and therefore wished to support families and promote solidarity within the family so as to:

- strengthen the prominent role of families in preparing children for life in society,

- help families fulfil their function, particularly by reconciling professional obligations and family life,

- make society aware of its responsibility towards people who cannot rely on the support and protection provided by a family.

That is why, over the next few years, the CDCS will, through a new committee of experts, the Committee of Experts on Children and Families extend its thinking on child/parent relationships.[1]

The starting point for our discussions was that parents have a greater duty than ever to help their children overcome the constraints of modern life and set them on the right path. It is for parents to seek, together with their children, the best way to prepare their future. "Preparing for the future by preparing one's own future" means even more to those who are responsible for a disabled child, for a family that cannot be neglected. Many examples show that the need for proper parenting has never been so great as in these times of social and economic upheavals:

- Parents or the adults responsible for children often have difficulty in offering a stable system of values and bearings when faced with a changing society and changes in the family, sometimes even the instability of family structures, social isolation, poverty and social and/or health difficulties.

---

1. "supporting parenting in the best interests of the child"

118

- Working life is becoming increasingly demanding and employment is increasingly insecure or underpaid. Faced with stress and/or sometimes financial problems, parents encounter more and more problems in reconciling the constraints of their working life with their responsibilities towards their children. Moreover, lack of employment can, in some cases, lead to marginalisation and make families more vulnerable with negative consequences for the children.

- All of these factors can have consequences for the family unit, and in particular for the well-being and development of the children (separation, disputes, violence, ill-treatment, rudeness and delinquency, anti-social activities, drug addiction, eating disorders and at-risk behaviour, mental and physical health problems, gaps in training and learning difficulties for both the adult and the child concerned).

The parents of disabled children will doubtlessly identify with these examples, for disabled children often live in a family with their sisters and brothers.

You may think that I am painting a rather gloomy picture of the situation as many families - fortunately - live harmoniously. However, it was the CDCS' task to take stock of all the cases in which families and children are unable to develop their full potential, and to seek solutions to put an end to such situations. We therefore wish, among other things, to highlight:

1. the problems that children themselves may encounter, such as violence at home or in society, (corporal punishment or psychological violence at home, harassment by other children or young people at school or during leisure activities and violence communicated to children by the media),

2. prevention strategies for adults and children, particularly ways of helping families in difficulty so as to avoid the break-up of the family and assist parents and children in cases where protection measures, and sometimes placement, proves necessary.

119

In such cases, all family members - parents, single parents, parents-in-law, foster parents, brothers/sisters and grand-parents - have a role to play.

Avenues for future work

The Malaga Ministerial Conference on Disability (May 2003) once again showed that we need to adopt a common integrated approach to the issue of disabled children and adults in an integrated manner. One of the main challenges for these children is their integration as citizens and their participation in the decision-making process.

The Committee on the Rehabilitation and the Integration of People with disabilities (CD-P-RR) and the European Committee for Social Cohesion (CDCS) have already shown that they are capable of working together successfully.[1] I therefore see several avenues for future co-operation between these two committees as well as with the group responsible for drawing up the disability action plan:

1.   Reviewing and adapting the work already carried out by the Forum for children and families and adapting it to the specific needs of children with disabilities. I am thinking in particular of the activities carried out as part of the:

   i) project on "children, democracy and participation in society",

   ii) the debate and discussions on "psychological violence".

2.   Developing fresh co-operation, particularly through the activities of the Committee of Experts on Children and Families, which will hold its next meeting in December 2004.

At this meeting, the Committee of Experts will identify its priority activities for the 3 coming years in the light of the 28th Conference of European Ministers responsible for family affairs, which will take place in Portugal in 2006.

Subject to the approval of the Committee of Senior Officials, which has not yet met, parenting should be one of the subjects

---

1. See the MAUDINET report: "Access to social rights for people with disabilities in Europe", Council of Europe Publishing, Strasbourg, 2003.

of the conference. I believe it is important to take a look at the difficulties encountered by families which have a disabled child, families which often have only one parent because the other has abdicated.

These parents have many needs, particularly:

– the need for dialogue within groups where they can discuss their problems, exchange examples of good practice and help one another,

– the need for access to psychological support, to help them understand what has happened to them, for being the mother or the father of a child that is different from other children is a situation in which they did not expect to find themselves and which calls the structure of their family into question.

In France an experiment is currently being conducted which gives parents access to a medical consultation involving both a paediatrician and a psychologist. This provides care for the child and psychological support for the parents to help them overcome the shock they may have suffered.

Conclusions

By way of conclusion, I would like to pay tribute to parents who every day manage to find the considerable sum of energy required to bring up a disabled child. I would also like to underline the importance of the role of the associations which help these parents and their children to fulfil their potential and overcome the difficulties they encounter on a daily basis. I would also like to stress the importance of the work done by the staff of medical and social establishments: general staff, social workers, doctors, nurses, physiothera-pists, etc. And last but not least I would like to thank teachers who, on a daily basis, do everything they can to integrate chil-dren with disabilities into society. And despite all of this, a great deal still needs to be done. Thank you for your attention.

121

Assessing the potentialities of children with disabilities

Ms Aase Frostad FASTING
Specialist Clinical Psychology / Neuropsychology
Huseby National Resource Centre for Visual Impairment
Norway

Abstract

During the past 20 years the biological-medical interpretation of the concept of disability has been challenged by a bio-psychosocial understanding. The awareness of the link between a child's diagnosis, impairment or illness and psychological, social and educational factors is increasing.

The presentation will put focus on the consequences of this new awareness for the child, the family and the professionals and service systems. Our vision for children who have a disability is that they should have the opportunity to develop personally, participate in society and enjoy life in the same way as other children. How do we transform this vision into the practical life of a disabled child and his/her family? The question requires that we develop strategies and activities taking into account different fields and various levels. One challenge is building bridges between the medical services and special education support systems. Assessing the potentialities of children within a multidisciplinary model can provide a basis for individualized plans that include education and social support services, as well as health services and give suggestions as to special needs, teaching aids and facilities.

The main goal of an assessment is that it is to be used as a basis for intervention and as an educational guideline. The importance of close co-operation between parents and professionals in this process is strongly emphasized. The assessment of a child's functions and the content of an individual plan should be transformed into practice and promote the child's development and learning process. Our goal is to ensure that the child is offered optimal opportunities of development and participation and that the education promotes self-respect and independence in the child and is meaningful to the child's family.

Under the heading of a multidisciplinary model the presentation will describe how a child's functional abilities and potentialities can be assessed. The presentation will address the following questions:

- Why is it important to detect and define a disability and assess the child's functions and potentialities?
- What do we assess?
- How do we do it?
- When do we do it?
- Who has the responsibility?

The Norwegian model of the responsibilities of the municipalities, multidisciplinary teams within the specialized health system as well as the educational system will be briefly described with some final remarks as to the challenges of this system.

Presentation

Ladies and gentlemen – dear collegues! During the past 20 years the biological-medical interpretation of the concept of disability has been challenged by a bio psychosocial understanding. The awareness of the link between a child's diagnosis, impairment or illness and psychological, social and educational factors is increasing.

What does this new awareness mean in practice for the child itself, the parents, professionals meeting the family and for the service systems? Certainly, this understanding calls for actions to build bridges between the medical service systems, multidisciplinary teams and the support systems for special education. It is of vital importance for the disabled child and the family that the health system, educational system and social support services can see the child as a child, with potentials for development, like any other child, and that the professionals involved in these systems engage themselves

123

together with the parents in the task of transforming the visions of equal opportunities, participation and inclusion to practical realities for each child.

Assessment of the functions of a child with a disability is, of course, complicated by the dynamic nature of child development, sometimes also by the child's medical condition. Most disabled children have been in contact with doctors and hospitals in the diagnostic process. A functional assessment should take place as part of the diagnostic process or as soon as a child's medical condition is stable. This is a period when parents ask some important questions as to how the child will develop? Will he/she be able to walk? Will he/she be able to talk? How will he/she manage school? What can we do to support her/him and promote her/his development? Parents think far ahead about a possible future of their child. These questions are difficult to answer correctly. Nevertheless, parents should have the possibility of discussing these questions and their worries with a professional who has time enough to listen to the questions and discuss the worries, even if the specialist does not have exact answers to all questions.

In this presentation I shall describe some challenges related to the link between diagnosis and development of disabled children. Under the heading of a multidisciplinary model and assessment of the potentialities of the child I shall address the following questions:

- Why is it important to assess the potentialities of a disable child?
- What is the purpose of an assessment?
- How can an assessment be used as a basis for individualized planning?
- What do we assess?
- When should the child's development and functions be assessed ?
- Who is participating at the assessment, where does it take place?
- A final question: Does it work?

124

Finally, I shall briefly describe the Norwegian model of multi-disciplinary teams established in the specialized health system as well as in the educational system, both systems within the mainstream structures and with the main objective to provide support to disabled children and their families. I shall make a few comments as to the importance of competence and research. But now to the first question:

Why should we assess the potentialities of a disabled child, what is the purpose?

The purpose of an assessment can be defined as a need to do registrations and collect detailed information on this particular child's functioning in relation to various tasks and situations. Which learning strategies, compensatory and coping strategies does the child have at this stage of development, which interests and support needs does he/she have. The aim of the assessment process is to understand the child's needs and use the information as a basis for an educational plan for the coming year. Individualized planning is a basic principle in the Norwegian efforts to meet the support needs of a disabled child and his/her family. An individual plan includes assessment of needs in several areas, one area being the educational plan.

The recognition and definition of a learning disability, for instance, are necessary and contribute to our understanding of the basis of the problems in a child's educational, developmental and social progress. For a child with special instructional needs, knowledge about the child's visual function, mental and behavioural functions, as well as language comprehension, learning style and capacity is important. One must consider environmental factors and the need for teaching aids, technical aids and social support as part of this planning. Without such knowledge we do not have a basis from where we can design the education plan according to each child's needs.

Regardless of labels such as mental retardation, deafness, blindness or cerebral palsy, all children who have special

125

educational needs also need much the same carefully planned steps in learning how to solve problems, understand the surrounding world and interact with others. A careful analysis of learning strategies to help the child develop and use her learning potentials is important. To give advice and help parents and teachers to understand the child's learning style and capacities is part of the assessment process. Participation and equal opportunities for a disabled child does not merely mean to be there – in the class with the other children. It means to be present and included as an individual with her strengths and weaknesses. The teacher needs to know which goals and measures are important for this child, and have available teaching aids and technical aids appropriate to help this child develop and learn, like all other children. The challenge for the school is to promote the child's learning process, as well as supporting the child in developing self-respect and self-confidence and avoid so-called learned helplessness.

Continuously experiencing failure related to school tasks, will cause any child to lose interest and motivation towards the tasks. This will not promote development of coping strategies for the child. To put a child in front of tasks impossible for him to deal with and without adequate instructions is not a learning situation. To experience success and to feel capable and able to cope are strong motivational factors for any child in a learning situation. A disabled child may often, when comparing himself/ herself to other children, feel that he/she is not succeeding. For any child it is of vital importance that he/she experiences success in relation to the individual tasks and challenges he/she is presented. The child's interest in, or reactions to school-tasks and the social context he/she is operating in, should continuously be observed and evaluated in the school setting, but should also be evaluated with assessments to check the quality of the individual plan. If we observe that the child is not attentive or motivated when facing a task, we should reconsider the content of the task, reconsider the environmental support or question the content of the educational plan and the learning situation.

126

How can we assess potentialities of a disabled child?

A developmental screening or assessment typically takes place during the first years of the child's life. In the resource centre where I work we often see and assess children's functions just a few months after birth. If parents or a doctor suspect that a child may have a visual impairment, the child is first seen by a local eye doctor and may then be referred to a multidisciplinary assessment at the centre where I work. In approximately 70% of children with visual impairments, the etiological history includes not only eye, but also brain pathology. A multidisciplinary developmental assessment is therefore necessary to understand this complexity. A developmental assessment is something different than a traditional intelligence test, but we can use some of these tests for our assessment purposes, not as intelligence tests, but to draw up a profile of the child's functions in several areas. It is important to notice that the test results of a small child are not prognostic of its intelligence. It is a measure of the child's development and functions at the time of testing and a good starting point with guidelines for intervention and support.

Assessment measures and tests are selected on the basis of the child's age, the likelihood that the questions we have will be answered, and the ability of the child to master the test requirements. Tests should be chosen that balance a child's strengths and weaknesses. Screening instruments will of course be inadequate in capturing the complex nature of the child's functioning, and selecting items that are sensitive indicators of disabilities, as well as potentialities of the child is a challenge.

The assessment process begins even before direct contact with the child. A thorough history review of the child's medical and developmental history before the formal assessment is advantageous. The diagnosis or medical etiology is a significant element of the story and sometimes carries implications in terms of prognosis, development and behaviour. The parents have a right to get the information they wish related to these issues and be supported in their efforts to raise their child to live with his/her disability. The history should be

127

obtained by a personal interview with the parent, by having the parent complete a questionnaire, by direct contact with the referring professional and/or by chart or records review.

In Norway most children – disabled or not, are enrolled in nursery school. Children with special needs have a legal right to enter nursery school, as they also have a legal right to education based on his or her specific needs. This means, among other things, that the child also has a right to receive specialized teaching aid according to his needs. Consequently the most important question when a disabled child enters nursery school is: which are this particular child's special needs? An assessment should give a detailed answer to this question.

What do we assess?

An assessment should be worked out in co-operation with the child's parents, and must include an interview of the parents about the child's development so far. Which goals for their child are important for the parents, how do they see the child, what questions do they have. Parents often worry about the child's development and progress and may also worry about the child's emotional situation. Even if most parents know that they are the best experts at understanding and supporting their child as compared to other caretakers, they often feel that they do not do enough or understand enough. Parents often ask for their child to be referred to a multi-disciplinary assessment because they wish to have specialists help them presenting the child's potentials and needs to the municipal authorities. They also wish to discuss the child's development and what to expect of the child at the stages of development, or in the future. The medical history as the parents understand it, may be of importance because the parents' expectations towards the child may be coloured by this understanding. Also the child may ask questions about his/her impairment or disability, and parents often feel that these questions are difficult to answer, because they do not have a good enough understanding themselves, often because of lack of information.

A developmental screening or assessment includes tasks of mental functions, motor functions, social functions and behavioural functions. Through observation or registration of the child's ways of solving various play-like tasks presented to the child, we obtain a picture of the child's communication and coping strategies and her preferences of activities under various conditions. A professional observer can utilize this information to draw a profile of the child's potentialities, his/her stronger and weaker functions. To collect information of the child's strategies of learning and coping and how the child naturally compensates for her difficulties is basic in supporting the child's development. To communicate is a fundamental need in any child. All children, even if they have a severe and complex disability have a potential for communication and development. If the child's impairment puts restrictions on his ability to communicate because of speech and movement difficulties, a trained multidisciplinary team will through analysis of the child's behaviour, responses and body language be able to give advice on how to support the child's interaction with others. Through adequate strategies, teaching aids and technical aids a child can compensate for difficulties he/she may have in making himself/herself understood by others.

When should we assess?

As mentioned, an assessment typically takes place during the first years, and should be repeated at certain stages of development. The main reason for this is the need to evaluate the effect of the educational programme as well as the child's reactions to it. As years go by, the expectations from the school, as well as the child's individual development changes, and consequently assessments should be repeated several times, particularly in connection with shifts of level (from nursery to primary school and to secondary school).

Who should participate in assessing the potentialities of a child who has a disability? Where does it take place?

Obviously, children with, for instance, cerebral palsy, who often have a complex disability and may have movement as

129

well as cognitive, perceptual and language problems, should meet a multidisciplinary team with a physiotherapist, psychologist, special teacher, occupational therapist and a doctor. If the child has a visual impairment, the impairment may be caused by a cerebral dysfunction. Consequently, one should consider not only the vision of this child, but should assess functions like eye/hand co-ordination and movement, eye movements and various qualities of visual function as well as cognitive, hearing and language functions. A child with a more limited disability meets with a smaller team having the competence needed for each child's condition.

On the basis of the information we collect and common knowledge of the disability in question, we take actions to teach the parents how they can discover and support the child's potentials and needs and prevent development of additional problems.

As a rule, the assessment takes place within the system of so-called mainstream structures. The municipal health service system and the local educational psychological service are the primary carers. For a child with particular special needs the local services may refer the child to the specialists within the health or education system at the county level. For a child with a rare or complex condition it may be relevant to refer the child to specialists at the regional or national level. Conclusions from assessments of the specialists at the various levels are reported to the municipal or local carers, so that they can use these conclusions in their further efforts to promote the child's development and support the family.

The Norwegian National Support System for Special Education

As of 1977 the legislation regulating the educational rights of children in Norway has had as its main intention that children with special needs, regardless of the degree of the child's disability, have a right to special education based on their needs, in their local school, together with all other children in his local community. We have very few special schools or special classes in Norway. The legislation emphasizes that special

130

education before and after compulsory school age should be provided for all children who will benefit from such support. The formerly existing special schools have over a period of 15 years been transformed to a national support system for special education with 31 national and regional units and multidisciplinary teams. The responsibilities of the municipality on the areas of education, social and health services are defined, and every municipality has a local educational psychological service. This service is responsible for the documentation of the special needs of a child, and they do so by assessments of needs and potentials. If these authorities need counselling or support from a specialized team in their work with a disabled child, the regional or national support system will provide such services after referral. The specialists will help increase the level of competence at the municipal level. When referring a child for multidisciplinary assessments of functions, the parents, special educators and teachers from nursery schools or local schools most often accompany the child at the examination or assessment. They are of course important sources of information as well as recipients of information, knowledge and ideas that will benefit the child.

Public health services

Public health services are organised in a three-tiered system. As in other areas, the aim is to decentralize as much as possible in order to create the shortest possible distance between provider and patient and each of the 435 municipalities has its health service system according to the Local Health Care Act, passed in 1984. The philosophy behind this is that decentralization is an expression of applied democracy. The Act on patients' rights, passed in 2000, represents a reform of the health legislation and has as its main elements a right to choice of hospital and a right to treatment. In addition to these rights, the act concerns information, access to medical journals and the need for patients' informed consent to treatment. The patient is to be treated as an equal party in the relationship with care providers. This, of course, goes for parents of a disabled child as well. Many children with disabilities need no

131

particular attention from the specialized health system. Quite a few children have, however, complex and severe disabilities and need regular attention from medical doctors of various specialities, as they do from other professionals, such as physiotherapists, occupational therapists, nutrition specialists, speech therapists and psychologists. The goal of such attention is provision of necessary specialist assessment and treatment and measures to support the child develop its potentialities as a supplement to earlier obtained knowledge. Such help is to be described in the individual plan of the child.

My final question is: does it work?

Does the described system meet the needs of disabled children and their families? Does it work? To this question I have to answer yes and no. The Norwegian example is an ambitious one. A decentralized service system requires systematic co-ordination of all elements and necessitates that all actors involved with the child have knowledge of each other and of the recommendations made. This is a huge challenge. Many families with disabled children feel that they act as co-ordinators in this complex service system and find this situation hard to handle. We have a considerable potential for improvement in this area. Our challenge is to work together as multidisciplinary teams, across professions and institutions, and that the result of these efforts is in accordance with the needs of the family. Responsibility and roles must be clearly defined related to all areas and types of services.

The level of competence related to complex and rare conditions and disabilities is most often too low at the local level. Without the support and counselling provided from specialists located at county, regional and national level, parents may experience that the quality of services provided is too low. Sometimes parents report that local authorities wait too long before they refer the child to the relevant specialists.

Speaking of competence and knowledge we have several challenges for the future. We need to increase our knowledge about strategies and measures promoting development and participation of children with various kinds and degrees of disability. New knowledge should be developed within a multidisciplinary setting and research, and through participation in international associations and networks. In all professional fields in Norway, we have over the years been interested in and taken advantage of knowledge and theories developed in Europe and the USA. Norway is a small country and we often look to other countries in Europe to increase our competence in many fields. In the field of rehabilitation and special education, for instance, the work of Alexander Luria and Lev Vygotsky from Russia in the seventies and from the Petø Institute in Hungary/Austria have had a great influence on assessment methods, as well as on models of rehabilitation and education in Norway. Our university students learn about these contributions. Collaboration and influence from our Scandinavian neighbours has been substantial, as well as influence and benefit from the work of colleague professionals in several other European countries. Therefore, one can say that the influence from Europe within various fields have been of great importance in the process of developing the Norwegian model. It is important that we continue to share experiences and that we learn from each other's good examples throughout Europe. A mutual challenge is that through this we transform the knowledge and contribute to improvement of care and support for disabled children and their families.

Challenges for families taking care of disabled children

Mr Berger HAREIDE
Deputy Director General
Directorate of Children, Youth and Family Affairs
Oslo, Norway

Abstract

Originating from a parent-initiative a series of three projects have been taken care of by Modum Bath Family Relations Centre, where the author was a director for 8 years.

133

In a deinstitutionalised Norway, where almost all disabled children grow up and live at home until they are young adults, it is of utmost importance to support the parents in their parenting work. Without active and co-operating parents, it will be difficult to promote inclusion and have full citizenship as a realistic goal for disabled children. And one of the most predictive factors behind the parenting quality is how the parents can co-operate and how their couple relationship is.

The first of the three projects was a research project – an attempt to acquire a close look at how the parents of disabled children experience their marital relationship. 17 couples were interviewed. Four of them were divorced. We had couples with children from the age of five to forty. We met them on average five times through a period of approximately two years. Each interview lasted 2-3 hours. The methodological approach was qualitative and narrative. We wanted their stories about the child – how it was to have the child, to live with him or her, and eventually let the child go. We wanted to learn about their co-operation with the professional helpers, how their family network was, how having a disabled child affected the relationship to the non-disabled siblings, and how they experienced grief, joy and meaning. And in all this: how their marital life affected, and was affected by, this life situation. The disabled child was number one on the priority list, the couple relationship ended up at the bottom, although they admitted that their relationship was crucial in how they managed the daily stress. This project has given us an indispensable knowledge base – directly from the parents – about their lives, and the critical factors needed.

The second project consisted of six one-week courses for parents, hosted at our centre. The courses actually lasted five days – from Monday morning until Friday afternoon, and the couples came without the children. The days were organised around three components: psycho education, counselling and recreation. The project was funded by the Ministry of Social Affairs.

In a way the one-week courses were a little exclusive. There were not many parents from the target group who would have a chance to participate. We therefore looked for some wider outreach measures, which then appeared in the third project. This chance appeared in 2002 when the Ministry of Children and Family Affairs asked our centre to run a three-year national project, aimed at relationship and communication enhancement and divorce prevention, for parents with disabled children. The project had a duration from 2002 to 2004, and was baptised "What about us?" – almost an exact quote from some of the parents. Our centre received an annual government grant of 4.5 million NOK to run the project. After 2004 it will become a permanent programme, administered by the Directorate of Children, Youth and Family Affairs. The commission was to contribute to a competence build-up focused on the problems met by parents when they have a disabled child. The project leaders were asked to develop, test out and evaluate specially designed couple workshops in formats of one day or a weekend. After an initial phase these workshops were supposed to be disseminated all over Norway. The project also has represented a special challenge for the 65 Norwegian family counselling offices, which were supposed to have a special responsibility in initiating these workshops.

The three projects will be presented and future implications will be discussed.

Presentation

Introduction: A late Saturday night

The whole thing started with some small talk a late Saturday night at a seminar after a delicious dinner. We were drinking coffee, and it was a relaxed and friendly ambience in this group of seminar committee members and me as the seminar leader. We had finished a long day in a weekend workshop where the topic was co-operation between parents and professional helpers. The participants were mainly parents of disabled children, and a few health professionals.

My background was a long life as a school psychologist, also working with families with disabled children. After a few

135

years as a college associate professor I had just started as a director of the Family Relations Centre (in Norwegian: Samlivssenteret) at Modum Bath Clinic and Resource Centre.

The committee members were curious about what kind of family relations centre this was. When I told them that we primarily had an outreach kind of work on how to strengthen couple relationships, they spontaneously asked me to come back next year to give them as couples a workshop. "We always have to focus on the disabled child. No one asks us how this is for us, and how we can survive as couples."

This conversation actually started three projects. Before coming back next year to this parent organisation, a research project had been initiated. There was a lack of knowledge in this field. Two years later a series of six one-week courses for parents were administered at our centre. Both projects were funded by the Ministry of Social Affairs. In 2002 the Ministry of Children and Family Affairs asked our centre to run a three-year national project, aiming at relationship and communication enhancement and divorce prevention for parents with disabled children.

In short, what we have experienced through these three projects is that working with the parents of disabled children in many ways presents a necessity if the aim is to promote inclusion and human rights for disabled persons. In a deinstitutionalised Norway, where almost all disabled children grow up and live at home until they are young adults, it is of utmost importance to support the parents in their parenting work. And one of the most predictive factors behind the parenting quality is how the parents can co-operate and how their couple relationship is.

1. The research project: 19 families

The first of the three projects, the research study, was an attempt to acquire a close look at how the parents experienced their marital relationship. A female family therapist, Kjersti T. Rogne, and I interviewed the parents of 17 "children" from the age of five to forty. Four of the couples were divorced. For two of these couples the interviews had to be conducted individually, or together with the new spouse. We therefore actually had a project involving 19 families. We met the parents on average five times through a period of approximately two years. Each interview lasted 2-3 hours. The methodological approach was qualitative and narrative. We wanted their stories about the child – how it was to get the child, to live with him or her, and eventually let the child go. We wanted to learn about their co-operation with the professional helpers, how their family network was, how having a disabled child affected the relationship to the non-disabled siblings, and how they experienced grief, joy and meaning. And in all this: how their marital life affected, and was affected by, this life situation. The material has been presented in a report from the Family Relations Centre, called "The time together must be robbed", referring to the fact that in the daily life there was very seldom time for just the two together. The disabled child was number one on the priority list, the couple relationship ended up at the bottom, although they admitted that their relationship was crucial in how they managed the daily stress. This project gave us an indispensable knowledge base – directly from the parents – about their lives, and the critical factors needed. A few conclusions from the findings will be presented:

The first phase – and the helping professionals

Many of the parents had received the message at the hospital that something was wrong. Their experiences were strikingly similar. There were many stories about how awkward or helpless the professionals were at this stage. It was for example quite unusual that both parents received the message together. What the parents most strongly missed, was someone there who could have enough time for them.

Some parents came home with what they thought was a healthy child. In spite of this some still had a suspicion that something was wrong. It was hard to live with the uncertainty and not having their worries eased. There were, however, a few positive stories from the youngest couples about how they were met by the health professionals.

In the report there is an extensive list of good ideas from the parents about what is important when a difficult message needs to be conveyed to parents. There is also a discussion about how the couple relationship was affected through this first stage. It was a challenge to handle one's own personal reactions, and at the same time care for the spouse. It was helpful both for the marital and family life when they were able to share. A common denominator in the divorce families was that the father did not take his part in the daily care.

When life goes on as a help receiver

One fact that was often mentioned by the parents was that there were marked differences in how the local municipalities offered support. This actually influenced the parents' decision about where they could live. The report lists what kind of support the parents regarded as crucial.

One common experience was that the parents always needed to be up front. They needed to think beforehand and be ahead of the professionals when a transition came up, for example when the child moved from kindergarten to elementary school. When the child reached the late teens or young adulthood, there was an especially vulnerable transition about moving away from home and to the young person's own apartment. It was hard to let go for the parents.

Receiving public support did something with the parents. Many described it as if they gradually got a lower self-esteem or lost their dignity. There was a marked difference between the generations of parents in this respect – from the youngest parents in their twenties up to those in their seventies.

The couple relationship was also drawn into this field, and had to carry a lot of issues that did not directly relate to their relationship. It was quite common to see projections: frustrations because of the lack of support from the municipality was easy to pour out on the spouse. Differences in opinion or attitude could then be vulnerable and they could easily hurt each other.

Daily life, house chores and gender roles

In earlier research about parents with disabled children there has been seen a marked gender difference in the daily life, with the mother as the main caregiver, and the father as the breadwinner. Not so much here, except for the oldest generation. The share of child care and house chores was quite equal between the mother and father. The father did, however, get more positive response from family and friends for what he did (no big surprise?). Although the practical work was quite equally shared, there was consistently a stronger sense of responsibility and engagement from the women: they were thinking more ahead, they worried more, etc.

In the report all the "heavy" aspects of the family life with a disabled child were summarized. The negative patterns in the couple relationships could also represent a vicious cycle. Time and energy was seen as a necessity to nourish the marital life, and a good couple relationship made the daily life easier and simpler for them.

Family and friends

There were many stories about how it had been for them to tell their parents about the child. The reactions were very different. The first reaction was often quite decisive in how the continued relationship developed. Often it ended up as either/or close or distant.

The relationship to their friends also could be quite an emotional issue. Many parents experienced a reduced social radius, and they admitted that they could be very vulnerable to how other people reacted to the child. This also was the experience with the neighbour networks.

Almost all the parents in the study were working outside the home, and experienced this fact as important and positive. The work place was a "normal" setting, a place where they had a "free" place away from all the extraordinary in the family life.

139

The study showed how the vulnerability in the social contacts also could affect the marital relationship. When the couple had different reactions to friends and family, or different needs of social contact, this could represent a strain on the relationship. But there were also examples of how social estrangement could also bring couples closer to each other.

The other children

In many families with disabled children there has been a role distribution where the mother takes care of the disabled child, and the father of the other children. This was more of an exception in our study. Both parents were thinking a lot about how it affected the siblings to have a disabled brother or sister. They experienced the gap between ideals and realities. It was not as easy to take care of the brothers and sisters as they wanted, and they regretted the fact. In the report there were many examples of how the daily life was influenced by this.

Grief – or not?

A sense of grief was often brought up in the interviews by the parents. There was a wide variety in how they experienced the grief. Some talked about how they had to bury the child they had hoped for, before they could accept the child they had actually got. Some described the grief as never ending. But a few parents did not recognise the topic of grief.

Joy – and meaning

There was also a deep sense of joy in the parents' lives, although they admitted that it often had to do with the small joys of daily life. As to the question of meaning, there were different views. Some had a conviction that there was a deep meaning underneath all that had happened. Others found it completely meaningless. Most of the parents differentiated between the meaningless in the fact that the child was disabled, and all the positive that the life with this child had given them. When they had a shared sense of joy and meaning, it also was nourishing for the marital relationship.

140

Two conclusions were finally presented from the study: 1. The necessity of getting practical support to sustain a normal life. 2. The importance of focusing on the couple relationship.

2. The 6 one-week courses: 38 couples

The second project was the one-week courses for parents, hosted at the Family Relations Centre. The courses actually lasted five days – from Monday morning until Friday afternoon, and the couples came without the children. The days were organised around three components: psycho education, counselling and recreation.

The psycho educative part was a workshop on issues that are important for couples in their marital life, like: expectations, communication, conflict resolution and commitment. The curriculum for this was taken from the research-based couple programme PREP (Prevention and Relationship Enhancement Programme), which the Family Relations Centre introduced in Norway in 1999. In addition, there were also topics included that are important for parents of disabled children, e.g. how it was to have a disabled child, how everyday life was for them, the relationship to the professional helpers, the family network, the siblings, grief and joy, and the life phases.

The counselling part was an offer for each couple of three sessions with a family therapist during the week, if they wanted. Most of them did, in order to clarify some of the issues that were activated through the workshop.

The third part of this, the recreation, was also important. Some of the couples were quite fatigued when they arrived. Through the week they had plenty of time to sleep (we always started late in the morning), to go for long walks in the woods, and to enjoy the cultural programme that was also a part of the course.

The Family Relations Centre had funding to host six courses in 1999/2000 for 6-8 couples each time. The courses were thoroughly evaluated, first immediately after the week and then with a follow-up four months later. The feedback from the parents was very, very positive. But the project has since been

141

put aside, because it has not yet found a permanent public financial plan, which also needs to include free leave from work to make it accessible for all who need it.

In a way the one-week courses were a little exclusive. There were not many parents from the target group who would have a chance to participate. There was therefore a need to look for some wider outreach measures, which then appeared in the third project.

3. The national initiative: a three-year project

The three-year national initiative from the Ministry of Children and Family Affairs, aimed at enhancing communication, strengthening relationships and preventing divorce in families with disabled children. The project had a duration from 2002 to 2004, and was baptized "What about us?" – almost an exact quote of the parents I first met. It was commissioned to the Family Relations Centre, and got an annual government grant of 4.5 million NOK. After 2004 it is expected to become a permanent programme under the Ministry of Children and Family Affairs, and administered by the Directorate of Children, Youth and Family Affairs in Norway.

The commission was to contribute to a competence build-up focused on the problems met by parents when they have a disabled child. The project leaders were asked to develop, test and evaluate specially designed couple workshops in formats of one day or a weekend. After an initial phase these workshops were supposed to be disseminated all over Norway. The project has represented a special challenge for the 65 Norwegian family counselling offices, which were supposed to have a special responsibility in initiating these workshops. That is why the project organisation both had a central staff at the Family Relations Centre, and also two regional family therapists working part-time for the project in each of the five Norwegian regions. One of the project goals has also been to establish and improve the co-operation with other institutions (hospitals, rehabilitation services, educational services, etc.).

142

So far, almost half into the third year, the workshop programmes have been developed, evaluated and refined, both
for the one day and the weekend format. The workshops have
been established in all five regions in Norway. The feedback
so far has been very positive, and there is growing demand
for a follow-up or booster session. In the competence programme more than 100 family therapists have gone through
the three-day courses for workshop leaders arranged in all
regions. More than 900 professionals from co-operating institutions have participated in shorter competence build-up
courses. In a two day national project conference early in 2003
there were 240 participants. A national network of co-operating institutions and parent organisations as well as equivalent
regional networks have been established. There has been an
active media coverage, and the general public now seems to
know a lot more about these issues.

4. Epilogue

Eight years have passed since that Saturday night with the parents in the committee. A lot has happened. I think the basic
idea underlying the three projects, the idea that has helped to
make them fairly successful and sustainable, has been to listen
to the parents and let their voice be heard and let them have a
say in what should be done. If we miss this bottom-up dimension in our work, we will also easily miss the human rights perspective. And we will not be on the road toward inclusion.

The parents' perspective

Ms Marchita MANGIAFICO
Vice President of the
National Parents Society for Persons with Disability
Malta

Abstract

Ms. Mangiafico is a full-time single parent of two children,
Sebastian (Seby) who is 17 years old and has cerebral palsy

143

with profound and multiple learning disability, and Vanessa, who is 14 years old. Ms. Mangiafico, has been actively involved as a parent advocate and public speaker for the past 5 years, elected twice on the board of the school council as a parent representative and elected to Vice-President to the National Parents Society for Persons with Disability.

The presenter will talk about milestones which have been reached in the Maltese system. Consideration will be given to the needs, support, education and financial structures which parents of children with disability face. The paper will also highlight the various benefits of services available such as respite services, community services, financial benefits and the needs of improvement for these services. Another issue to be discussed will be the ministerial responsibilities on persons with disability being a grey area.

The needs of families when a child is diagnosed with a disability are varied. Families are not taught how to live with disability but when all those involved accept that families do have an important role, if not the most important, in all the decision-making process this creates the greatest benefit for full inclusion of the child with disability within society and away from institutions.

Presentation

Thank you for inviting me here today. I am very honoured to be here and that I am given the opportunity to share my experience and perhaps my expectations with you all.

I am a single parent of 2 children, my son is 17 years old and my daughter is 14 years old. My son has severe cerebral palsy and is totally dependent. I have always cared for my children single-handedly. My husband left over ten years ago. My ex-husband and his family have never wanted any contact with the children. One of the main reasons for this is that our son's disability was never accepted in their family. They feel that it is something to hide.

I am Vice-President to the National Parents Society of Persons with Disability, elected council member to San Miguel School (Specialised School), facilitator for parental skills courses.

In Malta, the Equal Opportunities Act was unanimously voted for by ALL members of parliament in our country. We are very proud that all members of parliament agreed on this and passed it as the first law of the new millennium. It shows true commitment on behalf of the state. The National Commission for Persons with Disability (KNPD) was a set-up which, amongst other things, has to safeguard the rights of persons with disabilities. The rights of persons with disabilities are first and foremost the basic human rights of all and should not need to be differentiated. However, as parents and/or carers we have the right to safeguard that these rights are actually given to our children. Particularly, when these cannot speak for themselves. They are vulnerable and easily abused if the society they are in is not committed and sensitive to their needs.

Support: Early intervention is needed to guide parents, to provide them with information as this is not always given to them. Shock, grief, denial, anger will inhibit this process therefore it is important to have an ongoing source of contact and information which the parents should know of, for when they feel up to making the contact. Social workers in hospitals can be a good starting point. These can then refer to support groups of parents etc. My son was diagnosed at Great Ormond Street Hospital, London. I remember that the professional way in which the whole situation was handled has given me the courage to continue with my son's upbringing. Particularly I remember, the psychologist talking to me and saying that although the future may seem hard, most of the famous people that have made history, have had some form of "handicap". She said that Beethoven composed his best music when he lost his hearing. She hit it right on the spot, because Beethoven is my favourite composer. Then, I also remember, reading illegally through my son's file, and noticed that there was written what my daily behaviour was. At first I was offended, but reading it, I felt as though I was reading about another person. I was not aware that I was miserable

145

and crying most of the time. But then I said that I had to pull myself together and when my son was discharged from G.O.S Hospital, I felt ready to take what lay ahead.

So monitoring is important to see the parents' reactions and state of mind. This will enable the professionals to ensure that parents handle the new situation in a healthy supported manner. Of course the child is monitored closely too, having the parents well-being at heart ensures that the child is well taken care of.

Information: professionals need to include parents in discussions and decisions and use appropriate language and terminology that can be understood - no medical jargon and condescending attitudes. This will ensure that parents make the right decisions and develop a good attitude. A negative attitude from professionals may cause parents to close themselves in and avoid interactions which could lead to positive interventions. Why does my son's orthopaedic consultant keep insisting that because my son doesn't walk, he will definitely not consider operating? My son has both his hips dislocated. This is causing him great pain. The consultant sees him perhaps twice a year for ten minutes at the most. He never has any time to ask how my son spends his days and what he is capable of doing. He never wants to discuss the fact that due to his mistake, during a simple minor surgery to loosen my son's ligaments, his pain has increased. I had no support and could seek no alternative advice to make up for such a mistake. Luckily, the Paediatric Consultant introduced us to his registrar and he has made our life simpler. He dedicates enough time to listen to my fears and objectives for my son's future and is always there when I am meeting with other professionals to discuss my son's future. Decisions are taken together. This has helped me to continue believing in the medical professionals as a whole. Sharing of important and innovative technology and methods, ideals, to mention a few, improves the child's potential and future perspectives.

Social services: these need to be functional and person/needs-centred. A good social services set-up will facilitate the difficulties faced by families obtaining benefits, pensions,

146

entitlement for services and equipment, provision of appropriate housing and assistance this will help the family to
maintain a decent standard of living.

Support network: this is very important to ensure that families
function well, communities should have a strong inclusive
ethos and therefore aim at community services, In Malta,
being such a small country, a support network is easily created because usually families live in the proximity of one
another. There are others, though, who might find it difficult
because they feel that they are being judged for their performance with their disabled child. This is clearly observed when
they cannot cope with their children and would feel the need
to send the children to institutions or community homes. The
sense of guilt and failure overwhelms them and they usually
find themselves shutting off from the rest of the community.

Financial support: Extra costs are an added burden and therefore a good financial support system needs to be set up to
cover the extra expenses one way or another. In Malta we
have the Community Chest Fund which distributes public
funds collected purposely from the Maltese community, particularly during a Christmas Campaign, usually, creating a picture of pity of persons with disabilities to collect more money.
More than once we have tried to argue with the media that
persons with disabilities should be shown using their abilities
but some have argued that then money would not be donated
easily. I personally feel that the state should be the one to provide the expenses for these families and individuals as a sign
of commitment to their well-being.

Psychological assistance: Carers have serious decisions and
hurdles to overcome, sometimes even life and death decisions, decisions on surgery options, choice of therapy, financial burdens, e.g. change of lifestyle, possible change of
accommodation, choice of schooling, dealing with bureau-
cracy and lack of resources or services. Counselling and psychological intervention by professionals will ensure that
carers deal with these aspects in a healthy manner and that
they maintain good control over their emotions. They can

147

guide carers into leading a well-rounded life in order to ensure that burn-out is avoided and therefore carers are able to care for their loved ones for a longer time and in the best way possible to them. This is a service which is not readily given in Malta unless there is a life-threatening situation of risk of institutionalisation too late in our opinion. It would be better to prevent this from happening in the first place.

Support to siblings: Siblings undergo various changes and experience different feelings, sometimes they may feel neglected or unimportant. Helping them understand their feelings and learn how to cope in their reality will help them to grow and accept this, encouraging a positive attitude and eventual support from them towards their disabled sibling. I have seen many of my dear friends' children accusing their parents that they neglect them and only think about their disabled sibling. This has also happened to me with my daughter. She is always willing to help out with her brother and she is very kind and gentle, but she actually once told me that she is tired of having me dedicate most of our time to her brother. This has hurt me very much because where possible I have tried to give her enough time for her things. However, the older the siblings become, the harder it is to reach them, it seems that they have had enough of disability.

Housing: as previously mentioned, this is a great need, particularly when adequate accessibility is needed. Costs for homes are high, modifications are expensive, special equipment is extremely costly. In my particular case, I live in a first floor apartment. I carry my son 22 steps, at least twice a day. I am constantly arguing with the doctors because I should feed my son the appropriate food for him to put on weight. My argument is that he eats very well and very regularly but he should be on a gluten-free diet. The problem is that as soon as he eats the right diet, he will put on weight and therefore will make it difficult for me to carry him around. This will result in his confinement to his home. I am presently awaiting alternative accommodation but the waiting list is extremely long and I do not see any move in the near future.

148

Employment benefits: time off for special needs care over and above normal entitlement due to extra medical appointments and needs, therapy sessions, school appointments (MAPS, IEPS, etc.). Job sharing and flexible hours will ensure that the availability of carers to fulfil their job commitments will not hinder their performance. Providing these options will alleviate the burden and make it more cost-effective for employers too. I have been to may interviews to try and find employment and perhaps improve my family's standard of living but I have seen the interviewers' expression when I mention the fact that I have a child with a disability, followed by questions such as what will I do if my son is sick and who will care for him if I'm committed to work. Obviously, I have to be honest and say that I would have to care for him. So usually I am refused the job.

Inclusive day care facilities: in order to encourage carers to return to a normal lifestyle and maintain a good standard of living, it is important to offer support for them to return to their jobs. Therefore there needs to be the possibility of child care/nursery services, which will cater fully for disabled infants too, these need to be community-based for easy access. The financial aspect in this regard must also be considered. Presently in Malta, we have privately owned child care facilities which are costly and not always open to disabled children. State run facilities are just in their inception phase.

Community-services: avoid displacement problems as the child is familiar with the surroundings. As the community will have easy access to the family, a stronger bond is created and it is less likely for the family to become isolated.

Community homes and supported living: these will once again ensure that the family is not isolated and that the person with a disability will remain in her/his familiar environment.

Respite services: I am a great fan of them, otherwise I would not be able to be here today, because my son is being looked after at a respite home. These also provide much needed rest

149

for families. They can also provide a good opportunity for apron strings to be broken gradually and therefore facilitate transition to independence, thus providing space for the child to grow and mature, and for carers to know that they are in a safe environment. In Malta we have the Dar il- Kaptan and Arka Foundation in Gozo. These need to be adequately funded and resourced.

Post secondary facilities: the young adults have a right to further their education, continue developing, learn skills, find employment, continue in their journey of growth. These facilities will provide this and also allow the carers to continue with their lives rather than have to stop because their children have nowhere to go. This is when the young adults are at risk of being institutionalised unless other provisions are made. In 2 years time, I will be facing this nightmare because my son will be finishing school and with the Adult Training Centres (ATCs) in Malta, being extremely over-populated, he risks to stay at home. I also want to add that ATCs should be a continuation of the programmes learnt at school. There is a great gap as to what the education is providing for its' students and what the ATCs are doing for their service users. There is not enough funding to increase the resources needed to be able to create such an environment.

Employment: opportunities for employment of persons with a disability need to be made available and facilitated. Job coaches, training schemes and incentives for employers will ensure that this is possible. For parents this can be a cause of worry as it entails a number of factors, such as colleagues' support, ability to perform well etc. However, on the other hand it will put their mind at rest that their child will be able to be self sufficient and financially independent.

Direct payment scheme: ultimately the best way in which the real individual needs of the person with a disability and her/his family will be met. This way families and persons with disabilities can be in control of the services they need and of who they want to provide that particular service. They will be in control and be in a position to make the best choices for themselves. This of course needs to be a properly monitored scheme in order to avoid abuse by carers who try to take advantage of the individual's disability for their own benefit. Unfortunately, these cases do exist. Therefore, a monitoring body is needed. This is where we are at present in Malta.

Transition to adulthood: proper programmes need to be implemented; handover and continuity of teaching of skills are needed. Appropriate training of all staff concerned as well as the recruitment of various professionals needed is imperative, the individual needs of the persons with disabilities using these facilities need to be met at all times. Resources are also need to be made available. IT equipment, aids, etc. and ongoing teaching is vital. Personnel employed with persons with disabilities and their families ought to have clean police conducts, whether they have any tendencies towards alcohol or drugs, and provide appropriate references to be able to work so closely in the homes of persons with disabilities. Families need to feel comfortable with strangers coming into their homes and taking care of their children.

Special aids etc.: are presently partly-funded by the government. This is a means-tested procedure in general and one with a lot of bureaucratic processes but which does not yet fully alleviate the burden. It is a laborious journey where families need to fund raise if they are not in a position to personally cover the expenses which is hardly ever the case. This is a case of exposing the family's financial situation to outsiders and having to resort to charity. At present state services used by persons with disabilities invariably fall under the services for the elderly. This is not always acceptable and in the process of review. Ideally, there should be a cross-reference of all ministries with one particular one catering for the coordination of the services, needs, programmes, etc. of persons with disabilities.

All of the above situations require extra care and attention. This is why having a good social structure with adequate services and facilities is so important. It is already hard to cope with life when things are relatively straight forward and "normal". When there is disability in the family, it is therefore easy to understand how much more difficult, delicate and complicated things become. The family is at the mercy of resources and services which are particular and which are costly to run, therefore, at the mercy of governments and ruling bodies. If their priorities and commitments are not towards creating inclusive societies where individuals with disabilities can live in the least restrictive environments within their own communities and have equal opportunities and rights, then life becomes close to unbearable and therefore the disabled child is locked away from society, hidden at times even abused. Unfortunately, this seems to be still the case in some countries. It is our duty as citizens to ensure that this situation is eradicated completely. Last week, I was talking with another parent and when we were talking about what will happen to our children when we die, the conclusion we both came to, is that the options are that the children die before us or with us, because it's a shame that at this age and time, the set-up is not up to the standard therefore leaving parents of persons who cannot represent themselves without alternative options. In Malta, we are fortunate that the commitment by the state is in favour of inclusion and all it entails. The difficulties we are facing are due to financial limitations which do not allow us to continue developing at the rate we would like to.

Parents will always be parents and will generally always have their children's interest at heart, particularly when the child has a disability and when the child cannot represent himself/herself. Persons with disabilities have the right to live in the least restrictive environments. Respecting the parents and individuals themselves and including them in all decision-making processes ensures that these feel valued and contributes to their empowerment. Adequate services, benefits and schemes ensure that parents are involved longer in the raising of their children. Employment schemes for all ensure independence and self sufficiency. Those who cannot work still have a right to a good quality of life and to make choices.

All of these provisions will ensure that the individual with a disability is not institutionalised in large institutions but accommodated as long as possible within his/her own home and community. Institutionalisation should not be an option unless there is no other alternative available to the family. Parents who could not cope with the situation for one reason or another found great comfort in this set-up. Now everyone is aware of the need for reform and is in fact creating smaller units to encourage a more family-like set-up. In Malta we have 7 community homes, with smaller units, where everyone has his/her own bedroom, a communal kitchen and living room and en suite bathrooms. They use a person-centred approach. However, funding is very limited and expansion of services and homes is unfortunately at a standstill at the moment. There is still no set-up for those persons who need 24-hour care and are totally dependent.

The set-up of trustee funds that can safeguard the future of persons with disabilities and the provision of home-based services would be one of many solutions, however there must be a professional set-up of resources and qualified personnel which can be used. Ideally the set-up is in place and put in use long before the actual time of need so that we as parents can witness a smooth transition programme and be at rest that our children will be taken care of in the best possible manner when we are gone.

I would really like to see my son living in a community home where we can visit each other and spend days together, the same way as I envisage my daughter's future. I can't see my daughter living with me for the rest of her life. She needs to continue with her life and to make her own future and that is an option that I feel my son should have too, based on his individual needs. It is their right to independence, so there should be an option for these to move into their own home if this should be to their advantage. Therefore the set-up should be such that this will be a possibility.

153

SYNTHESIS

Report of Workshop 1: Desinstitutionalisation

Rapporteur:

Ms Elinor SUNDSETH
Director,
The Norwegian State Council on Disability
Oslo
Norway

Chair:

Mr Christian Boe KIELLAND,
Senior Adviser,
Ministry of Labour and Social Affairs,
Oslo
Norway

This workshop had 3 lecturers:

Prof. Jan Tøssebro, Professor of Social Work, Norwegian University of Science and Technology. He is also the chairman of the Norwegian State Council on Disability.

Ms Diana Hoover, Executive Director of the Mental Disability Advocacy Center (MDAC) in Budapest, Hungary;

Ms Bardhylka Kospiri, Advocacy Group Coordinator, Albania.

Prof. Jan T Tøssebro addressed the subject of Challenges of deinstitutionalisation during his presentation.

He described that despite changes in disability policy – and despite a widespread support for the ideals of inclusion in a number of countries towards more integration, inclusion and deinstitutionalisation - the inclusion policy meets both hesitation and criticism.

He referred to arguments presented against this policy, such as:

– that it is unrealistic;

– that mainstream services cannot possibly obtain the level of expertise found in specialized units;

– that inclusion can cause isolation, loneliness and other kinds of problems for vulnerable children.

Despite these obstacles and challenges - turning back to the time of institutions and segregation is, according to Prof. Tøssebro, not an issue.

As a strategy to identify the challenges, he discussed the following questions:

– What are the implementation practices?

– What happens and what are the challenges when inclusion policy is implemented?

– How do disabled children and their families experience the practice?

Prof. Tøssebro believes that international research on the subject of deinstitutionalisation can be divided into two distinct approaches:

One approach addresses effects by asking for example: do for example children learn more? Do they have a more positive self-image etc. in mainstream than in segregated settings? Findings from effect studies vary substantially and there is not enough scientific evidence to conclude that either of the types is better. This means that the choice between types to a large extent becomes a political or a value-based question.

The other approach is value-based. The participation of everybody is seen as a value in itself. The main conclusion from the value-based research is that inclusion reforms have led to significant improvements, but that there is still is a long way to go.

Because the Scandinavian countries - particularly Sweden and Norway – have some kind of pioneering status in inclusion policy, Prof. Tøssebro, has found it particularly interesting to study family experiences and current challenges in Norway. He presented data from a study following disabled children born 1993-95 as they grew up and from a study on intellectually disabled children at school.

Themes that were addressed were:

- family structure (for instance marriage and divorce, siblings and labour participation);
- pre-school services;
- inclusion at school and among peers;
- family experiences with services and support etc.

The studies show that:

- Large municipalities use segregation more than small ones;
- There is very little rejection of children in kindergartens;
- The segregation increases as the pupils/children grow older and get into higher grades;
- Special education in schools takes place outside the classroom;
- The professional strategy is one person or small-group-teaching;
- The disabled students in the classroom are taught or aided by non qualified assistants;
- The main challenge is how to develop a system where the children are taught by specialists (not by assistants) and in the classroom.

When it comes to the service system, parents find it satisfying when they have established access to it. The main challenge here is not the quality of the service but the access to it.

Ms Diana Hoover, Executive Director of the Mental Disability Advocacy Center, Hungary, talked about Deinstitutionalisation in central and eastern Europe.

We learned that the number of institutionalised disabled children has, in fact, increased in central and eastern Europe since the fall of communism.

The reasons according to Ms Hoover are:

- Economic upheavals as well as chaotic health system transition, from socialised to privatised systems;
- Families are without the necessary means to provide for vulnerable family members and have increasingly abandoned them to institutions.

Ms Hoover described most of the institutions in central and eastern Europe as being little more than warehouses:

- providing no rehabilitation and no means of ever being able to leave the system;
- many institutions in these regions have higher than average mortality rates. The residents are dying from malnutrition over long periods of time and from hypothermia;
- overuse of medications and abuse.

She pointed out several obstacles towards deinstitutionalisation, e.g.:

- resistance from institutions and psychiatrists (who receive funding by filling beds);
- widespread stigma against people with disabilities at political, professional, community and family levels;
- lack of trained staff in rehabilitation;
- lack of legislative frameworks allowing restructuring and financing of community-based mental health and social service systems.

To overcome these obstacles she mentioned a range of approaches, such as:

- piloting best practice community-based models;
- providing information about abuses in institutional systems to governments and media;
- directly challenging human rights abuses in institutions via the legal system;

– anti-stigmatization campaigns.

The Mental Disability Advocacy Center focuses on legal advocacy, litigation and law reform via national and international channels. The organisation calls for a ban of cage beds to reduce abuse of restraints. It is now initiating research into human rights abuses within guardianship systems. These systems currently allow many people to be detained and treated against their will.

Analysis in the light of international best practices and human rights standards will follow, as a baseline for advocacy at governmental and inter-governmental levels.

Ms Bardhylka Kospiri, Advocacy Group Coordinator, Albania, gave a presentation on challenging Human Rights violation of people with disabilities.

Ms Kospiri discussed the concept of disability and showed how disability occurs when:

– there is a gap or discrepancy between the ability of the individual and the demands of society;

– or when the consequences of the diversity of the population is not taken into consideration when designing and building society;

– therefore disability is not something individuals have, individual have impairments.

Her conclusion is that we live in a disabling society where some persons' practical living is limited due to the gap or discrepancy between their impairment and the environment or the demands of society.

In addition to the desire to have equal opportunities for taking part in the life of our society, the desire to break down the barriers that cause disability is also closely linked to ideas about the human rights of people with impairments. She referred to both the European Action Plan, the UN Convention, the Declaration on Human Rights, the European Social Charter, different EU treaties etc. as means for changing this.

Ms Kospiri suggested in her presentation that in eastern Europe people with disabilities face a higher degree of human rights violations in their every day life than people in the rest of Europe. This can be linked to the reforms creating market economies in central and eastern Europe which in turn have created new possibilities for most citizens and too often exclude disabled people. Their economic conditions are often harder than before and they have to fight for their survival.

Based on a survey completed by the Albanian Disability Rights Foundation (ADRF):

- 25% of people interviewed are affected by disability;
- a higher proportion of those live in chronic poverty, almost 60% live below the poverty level.

The basic cause of poverty for persons with disability is:

- exclusion from social, economic and political life;
- exclusion that leads to:
  - lack of resources
  - lower expectations
  - poor health
  - poor education;
- exclusion from mainstream social, economic and political opportunities, meaning lack of exercise of human rights throughout their lives. The result of this is that disabled people frequently fall further and further into chronic poverty and have little possibility to come out of this cycle.

Disabled children grow up being excluded from formal and informal education. This has an impact not only on qualifications and experience but also on levels of confidence and self-esteem. As a result later in life, they have restricted employment opportunities due to discrimination, lack of education, experience and confidence.

The Albanian Disability Rights Foundation (ADRF) is striving to ensure that human rights are respected for everybody, especially for person with disabilities.

160

Issues emerging in the ensuing discussion:

This workshop presented challenges of deinstitutionalisation with reference to experiences from Scandinavia and eastern Europe.

- The problems of countries with a stronger tradition of having large institutions were especially focused upon;
- It was questioned upon whether families in fact do have a real choice to take care of their children at home?

There was discussion about how parents with disabled children can be encouraged and enabled to take care of them at home.

How can obstacles to deinstitutionalisation be overcome, such as:

- resistance from institutions, from professionals, and from some parents or relatives who are unable or unsupported to face the challenge;
- widespread prejudice against people with disabilities amongst the population as a strong obstacle against living in the community;
- lack of functioning models of community-based rehabilitation;
- lack of trained staff;
- lack of legislative framework.

Examples of good practice, as presented by delegates, stressed that deinstitutionalisation should take place in stages. One step can be to improve institutions by downsizing them, decentralizing them, making them more home-like and integrating them in the community.

The other step, which should run in parallel, is to develop local, community-based services. The overarching aim, however, is to improve all services, inside and outside of institutions, through quality assurance.

Where do the member states go from here?

The results of the Conference should feed directly into the process of drafting the Council of Europe Disability Action Plan.

161

At pan-European level specific Council of Europe recommendations and guidelines are needed to promote community living for children with disabilities and to help families to take care of their disabled children at home in order to avoid institutionalisation. Those instruments should both be concrete and specific, but also flexible enough to be easily adaptable to all member states, taking into account their different backgrounds and circumstances.

Securing human rights and fundamental freedoms for everyone and arrangements for the full and effective implementation of all human rights must be applicable without any discrimination or distinction on any ground, including disability. Conditions for all persons with disabilities must be improved. But the participants especially stressed the importance to strive for the provision of equal opportunities for today's children with disabilities to participate in European society on an equal basis with other people.

Our challenge now is to transform our intentions into legal and political documents that will be our road maps for an inclusive Europe.

Report of Workshop 2: Disabled children and their families

Rapporteur:

Mr Hervé FACCHINI
Psychomotricien – Masseur – Kinésithérapeute,
Association Information Recherche (AIR),
Essert, France

Chair:

Mr Helmut HEINEN
Director,
Office for people with disabilities
German-speaking Community of Belgium

INTRODUCTION by Mr Helmut Heinen

Following the Malaga Conference, some countries had addressed the problem of disabilities by embarking on a process of deinstitutionalisation. The trend formed part of a broader, less medical approach to disability, which took greater account of the psychological and social aspects and involved the families of children with disabilities.

The western European countries were still looking for answers and Norway currently led the debate on the rights of families with a disabled child. Mr Helmut Heinen thanked Norway for taking this valuable initiative. This conference comes at a significant stage of the drafting of the new Council of Europe Disability Action Plan.

A time also significant because a number of Council of Europe member states have now begun a process of deinstitutionalisation, shifting from a medically-based approach offering assistance to a more open system of support catering for individual needs on the basis of the potential of persons with disabilities.

Furthermore, some 25 years after the introduction of various forms of deinstitutionalisation in western Europe, a large number of countries practising mainstreaming now face a tendency to trivialise disability and its consequences (this seems quite logical). They are endeavouring to find ways and means of improving service quality or bringing services into line with developments during the lives of children with impairments.

The Council of Europe's revised strategy for social cohesion in relation to the integration of children with disabilities

Ms Marie-Cécile Vadeau-Ducher, Chair of the European Committee for Social Cohesion (CDCS), Ministry of Employment, Labour and Social Cohesion, France.

Ms Vadeau-Ducher described the Council of Europe's activities and strategy and, in particular, the social cohesion strategy devised by the European Committee for Social Cohesion (CDCS) in relation to children with disabilities.

163

The Council of Europe and social cohesion

Ms Vadeau-Ducher said that human rights and, in particular, social rights had long been one of the Council of Europe's priorities. Since the Second Summit of Heads of State in 1997, social cohesion had been regarded as a key objective and become one of the main focuses of the Council of Europe's work. The aim was to promote a form of social cohesion based on human rights and a universal sense of responsibility. The European Committee for Social Cohesion had been set up after the Summit and had set itself four goals:

– to promote social cohesion in Europe;

– to uphold the social standards set out in the European Social Charter;

– to exchange information and good practice on social cohesion;

– to ensure that the European Code of Social Security was implemented and enforced.

The Third Summit of Heads of State would be held in Warsaw in May 2005 and one of its aims would be, in due course, to establish a European social model.

The Social Cohesion Strategy

The strategy had been devised in 2000 and revised in 2004 and made a declaration of intent, setting priorities for governments and the Council of Europe itself in relation to access to social rights in the following fields:

– social protection, housing and employment;

– urban social policy;

– the rights and protection of children;

– the rights and protection of dependent elderly persons.

Particular attention was paid to the rights and needs of vulnerable individuals and groups.

Lastly, the CDCS had launched work on the future of social cohesion by proposing the appointment of a group of wise persons to consider the future European social model.

164

The CDCS's activities in relation to children and families, particularly children with disabilities

The main problems encountered with children with disabilities were their integration and their adaptation to society (e.g. access to schools and the education system generally, from crèche to upper secondary school level, but also to employment) and access to special equipment and new technology. This created major problems for the children concerned and for their families, including:

- social problems, such as reconciling work and family life;
- financial problems, where health and equipment needs were not covered by state benefits;
- health problems resulting from mental strain and stress.

Until 2004, activities carried out through the Forum for Children and Families had concentrated on:

- day care for children;
- placing children at risk in institutions;
- children, democracy and participation in community life.

The Forum's discussions had focused on:

- the need to appoint a European children's Ombudsperson;
- the psychological violence and negligence to which some children were subjected;
- the abolition of corporal punishment in Europe.

Activities had also been aimed directly at families because this was the first setting in which a child experienced social cohesion. The main aims were:

- to strengthen the role of families;
- to assist families, particularly through help with reconciling work and family commitments;
- to make society take responsibility for persons who no longer had their family's support.

It was for parents to try to prepare their children's future, offer them a stable system of values and give them their bearings. There was a need to nurture and enhance parenting skills, to support families and parents' efforts on their children's behalf, to help the entire family to play its part, to prevent family breakdown and to support parents and children in times of difficulty.

Future courses of action for the European Committee for Social Cohesion

Various approaches were possible:

– to continue the work begun by the Forum and adapt it to the particular needs of children with disabilities;

– to establish new forms of co-operation through committees of experts on children and families, particularly in respect of parenting, which could be a major focus of activity, especially in view of the need to help and support families psychologically.

Ms Vadeau-Ducher concluded by paying tribute to the parents who put so much energy into caring for their disabled children. She also praised the relevant associations and their activities, the staff of the various medical and social establishments and teachers, while stressing that there was still a great deal of work to be done.

Assessing the potential of children with disabilities

Ms Aase Frostad Fasting, specialist in clinical psychology and neuropsychology - Huseby National Resource Centre for Visual Impairment, Norway

Ms Fasting described the type of assessment and operating methods that had been introduced in Norway, pointing out that although children with disabilities were often in medicalised surroundings, disability was not just a medical issue but one which related as much if not more to issues concerning the child's future and development, such as access to education and employment. These were not easy to resolve but children and their families had to be given the chance to discuss them.

166

Principles to apply when assessing a disabled child's potential

The key to the Norwegian approach was to gather as much information as possible about the child's capabilities through a tailor-made approach and personalised assessment, taking account both of the child's sensory tools and of his or her social environment. The aim was to devise an appropriate compensatory strategy – also tailor-made – to support and foster the child's development. Admittedly, disabled children needed an education adapted to their needs, but it was not enough for them to sit in a classroom with other children; they also had to take a full part in proceedings. The aim was not just to foster and facilitate learning but also to bring these children's self-esteem up to a satisfactory level, which could then be built upon. Accordingly, consideration would be given to educational content and the results obtained but also to the day-to-day experience of social and educational tasks, even if it meant rethinking educational content, teaching methods or the child's environment.

How to assess the child's potential

The starting point was a multidisciplinary assessment involving various professionals and the child's parents. Assessment was possible through the child's school and school medical service, particularly at primary school, but it could also be provided by specialists treating the child or, more generally, by anyone in the child's entourage.

Potential was measured in terms of sensory capabilities and cognitive and academic skills, taking account, of course, of the child's age. Attention was also paid to the child's motivation and, in particular, to communication and the development of systems of verbal and non-verbal communication and body language, which could be assisted where necessary.

These assessments were then sent to the municipal authorities so that they could adapt the measures taken, and, of course, to the child's parents.

167

The Norwegian system

There were few special schools in Norway, as the system was based largely on the specific principle that disabled children should be integrated into normal schools and the more general idea that, whatever a child's problems, all children had comparable needs.

The system was also based on ensuring as much decentralisation as possible in the link between providers and users. It was a complex system, in which the state, the counties and the municipalities all had a role. For example, although the state was involved, municipalities managed assistance for people with disabilities, as they ran the teams appointed to facilitate integration.

The system presupposed co-operation and co-ordination between all the specialists and professionals working in the field and the children's parents. Parents were therefore expected to co-ordinate arrangements – which was not always easy because the greater the disability, the more people were involved, and so parents complained that the assessment process was too cumbersome and, above all, too long.

Consequently, Norway was in the process of considering ways of improving its system for dealing with people with disabilities.

Mr Heinen highlighted the positive features of the Norwegian system, particularly the contribution and co-operation of all the professionals working directly with these children and the in-service training provided for them.

Challenges for families taking care of disabled children

Mr Berger Hareide, Deputy Director General, Directorate of Children, Youth and Family Affairs, Norway

Mr Hareide reported on a workshop involving the families of disabled children and in particular on a psychological support centre which had been set up for the children's parents. He was responsible for providing psychological back-up for the sixty or so families enrolled in the centre, and expressed some of his ideas about the functioning of the family unit when there was a disabled child and, in particular, the relationship between the parents. Addressing the issue of the integration and citizenship of children with disabilities also meant taking an interest in their families and making an effort to build up families' inner resources. When these families were interviewed, it became clear how much impact their child's disability had on them and how many repercussions there were. The effects varied according to the extent of the disability (ranging from minor handicaps to multiple disabilities) and depended on the parents' ways of expressing what was happening in their lives, their family and work relationships and their own attitude to the disability.

Mr Hareide's first point related to the parents' and the family's reaction to the diagnosis. This was often announced by a medical authority in a medical setting, and in a hurry, so that parents felt that their children were no longer in their hands, that they were being kept out of the picture and that they were not being given the full facts. Some consideration should be given to how health professionals should be announcing such diagnoses, although there appeared to have been some progress in this respect, as the experiences of the younger parents had seemed less negative than those of the older ones. It should also be a requirement for both parents to be informed of the diagnosis, not just one, who would then be expected to relay the news to his or her partner. This appeared to be a way of keeping couples united. The reaction to such diagnoses also varied according to the age of the parents involved. Often younger parents accepted the diagnosis without discussing it, whereas older parents reacted more defiantly, already thinking about the future and the difficulties to come. Diagnoses were also greeted differently by fathers and mothers – mothers were often more combative whereas fathers were more fatalistic.

Mr Hareide's second point concerned the need for families to reorganise themselves to cope with a disability. In Norway, it was most often the mother who did the bulk of the work entailed by the presence of a disabled child, sacrificing her job and handling the practical side of things. It was generally

169

mothers who would get up at night, for example. If the parents separated, tasks were better distributed, at least as far as practical chores were concerned. Quite clearly, this distribution of the tasks deriving from the child's disability caused friction between the parents.

The third point concerned the process of telling other members of the family about the disability. This was often accompanied by feelings of shame and awkwardness vis-à-vis other family members. Some, however, for example the disabled child's grandparents, showed signs of support. However, it was often the case that the family circle would gradually shrink and the family would feel cut off from the rest of society. It was an advantage for both parents to hold on to their jobs, as work colleagues also provided support. Lastly, it was important to remember to take account of other family members, particularly any brothers or sisters that the disabled child had.

In conclusion, it should be said that these parents were often heroic in their attitude and put in an enormous amount of effort, which the professionals and municipal authorities had a duty to acknowledge and support. They also had to learn to share the burden, however, organise themselves efficiently and reserve time for recreational activities together and with their other children, and they needed to be in a position to call on a therapist where necessary. One of the projects set up by the centre was based on training courses for parents of disabled children, which were held at weekends and focused on three main areas, namely the psycho-educational aspect, counselling and leisure time.

The parents' perspective

Ms Marchita Mangiafico, Vice-Chair, National Society of Parents of Disabled Persons, Malta

Ms Mangiafico described both her personal experience as a single mother raising two children, one of whom had cerebral palsy and the general situation in Malta. From what she described, a number of needs could be identified:

– the need to think about the way in which disabilities were announced to people: she stressed the need for professionals

170

to involve the parents, use simple language, avoid hiding behind medical jargon and take the trouble to explain and communicate, both when announcing the disability and throughout the process of caring for the child;

– the need for early, all-embracing action, both with regard to the rehabilitation process and in the form of psychological back-up: from the first day on, when they were faced with the shock of discovering that their child was disabled and the anger and the denial that this elicited, families needed support. Psychological back-up was vital for parents, the child concerned and brothers and sisters, who felt abandoned and had to be able to put what they felt into words;

– the need for financial and state backing;

– the need to set up small-scale, local care facilities and anticipate the time when disabled children would grow up by setting up facilities for disabled adults as well. Private services in Malta were expensive but they made it possible to organise family life more efficiently. However, after a time, the facilities petered out and the disabled child found himself or herself at home again;

– the need for specially trained professionals and workers.

In Malta, support was primarily provided by the public and could be somewhat pitying. It was preferable by far for assistance to be provided by a government body.

Financial support should cover the appointment of a third person to carry out day-to-day tasks. There was a limit to neighbourhood support networks, for example, which eventually gave rise to feelings of embarrassment and guilt.

Funds were also necessary for the adaptation of housing, as this often required changes which cost a substantial amount or posed logistical problems, as in cases where children had to be carried up several flights of stairs.

There was also a need for measures to enable parents to continue working, or for compensation for the loss of income brought about by the need to look after a disabled child.

171

Even if the parents had jobs, employers and the social security system needed to show more understanding when they were forced to be absent.

Mr Heinen highlighted the obvious special needs of people with disabilities and their families, which had been so clearly reflected in Ms Mangiafico's description of her experiences. He drew a parallel between her statement and Mr Hareide's research, which highlighted the efforts that were required of families and hence the need to help them at all levels, not least in order to offset the social and economic disparities occasioned by the arrival of a child with disabilities.

General discussion

Information about practices in different countries was exchanged and questions were put to the speakers.

Italy

Italy was concerned with improving parents' working conditions by giving priority to work close to home, flexible working time, authorised absences and a system of two years of early retirement which could be split up and taken according to families' wishes. Care facilities were available and it was compulsory, for example, for crèches to accept a disabled child at the family's request. Steps had also been taken to address the problem of the death of a disabled child's parents. For instance, Italian law granted three days per month of paid leave to persons within the third degree of kinship together with an orphan's pension for the disabled child. There was also a whole range of measures designed to improve the image of people with disabilities among employers and colleagues.

Denmark

Families had been the main focus of the speakers' contributions and the workshop but children themselves also had to be asked to express their views and their desires. Denmark was experimenting with gatherings of young disabled people designed to help them understand other disabilities and the prejudices that other people had about their own disabilities.

172

Encouraged to express themselves, disabled children had gradually been prompted to voice their own demands (for example, a sign language newspaper for the hard of hearing). This was reminiscent of Mr Hareide's experience although there were discussion groups for children and adolescents, not just for parents and families.

Bulgaria

Like many other countries which were carrying out a complete overhaul of their legislation, Bulgaria was finding it difficult to introduce reforms. Some consideration could be given to the role that the Council of Europe might play in helping to implement such reforms.

Overall conclusions

Through four very informative and moving presentations, the workshop had confirmed the need to take account of families when caring for children with disabilities.

The first speaker had stressed that social cohesion was one of the main focuses of the Council of Europe's work, which it carried out through the European Committee for Social Cohesion (CDCS). The interests of the disabled child were paramount, but children had to be with their families, which were the primary setting in which they experienced social cohesion.

The second speaker had described the approach adopted in Norway, where the system was based primarily on the integration of children with disabilities. Particular account was taken of their individual potential so as to help them to establish a place in their family circle and the education system. Accordingly, Norway had introduced a multidisciplinary disability assessment strategy, which offered assistance at various levels, but always involved families in the process.

The third speaker had described his experience of providing psychological support for families, especially through discussion groups for parents, which built up families' inner resources and enabled them to provide a home that was conducive to their disabled child's development.

173

Last of all, the contribution by a parent of a disabled child had starkly highlighted families' day-to-day difficulties, including financial, social, logistical and psychological problems, which confirmed the need to look after families just as much as their disabled children.

Providing families with technical, practical, financial and social assistance but also psychological support, was a way of helping disabled children to flourish in a context of social cohesion, while enhancing the image of disabled children in society.

Some recommendations for the Council of Europe Disability Action Plan

Mr Marc MAUDINET
Director
National Technical Centre for Studies and Research
on disability and social misfit (CTNRHI),
Paris, France

Abstract

This presentation is based on the report, "Access to social rights for people with disabilities in Europe". The general aim of that report is to highlight the fields of social activity in which access to social rights for people with disabilities needs special vigilance. The report was first presented in Paris in December 2003 at the French national closing ceremony of the European Year of People with Disabilities.

It maintains an impetus the Council of Europe has created in line with the principles underlying its work. Those principles recognise respect for fundamental rights and access to economic and social rights as prerequisites for development, social cohesion and democratic renewal. The backdrop to the report is the efforts to combat all forms of discrimination and the report describes:

– general principles and measures aimed at improving access to social rights for people with disabilities in Europe;

– the major obstacles they encounter in securing access to their rights as regards:

- social, economic and legal protection, housing, the built environment, urban life and transport,

- vocational training and employment, education, schooling and higher education,

- social participation, access to information, communication and new technologies,

- and health facilities and medical care.

This presentation is specifically concerned with the third part of the report, which ends with a series of recommendations for improved access to fundamental rights and social rights for people with disabilities.

Presentation

The base reference for this presentation is the report on "Access to social rights for people with disabilities in Europe". The general aim of that report was to highlight the areas of social activity in which access to social rights for people with disabilities requires special vigilance.

The report was first presented at UNESCO in Paris in December 2003, at the French national closing ceremony of European Year of People with Disabilities, and followed on from the Council of Europe report on "Access to social rights in Europe" by Mrs Mary Daly.

The report on "Access to social rights for people with disabilities in Europe" is a further advance in the movement set in motion by the Council of Europe and the principles underlying its action, principles that establish respect for fundamental rights and access to economic and social rights as one of the requisites for development, social cohesion and democratic renewal. The context of the report is the combating of all forms of discrimination and it sets out to identify principles and measures for improving access of people with disabilities to social rights in Europe and the obstacles substantially

175

hampering access to rights for people with disabilities in the spheres of:

- Social, economic and legal protection;
- Housing, the built environment, town life and transport;
- Vocational training and employment;
- Educative activities, schooling and higher education;
- Participation in society, access to information, means of communication and new technologies;
- Access to health systems and medical care.

This presentation focuses on the third section of the report, which concludes with a set of recommendations aimed at improving access of people with disabilities to fundamental and social rights.

1. Access of people with disabilities to social, economic and legal protection

More specifically regarding social protection, the following obstacles may be identified:

At political level:

- Lack of political commitment or an unstable political climate;
- A philosophy of centralisation in the national and regional administration, causing reluctance to delegating decision-making to local authorities;
- The structure of welfare systems;
- Unsuitability of procedures for effectively exercising rights;
- Opaqueness of laws and regulations.

At the administrative organisational level:

- Lack of clarity in action programmes (benefit, compensation - technical assistance, helpers etc.) on the part of the authorities, in design and launch phases and in their commitment to achieving the objectives set;
- Lack of suitable systems for feedback, supervision or effective budgetary checking for action programmes;

- Fragmentation of competence of administrative departments;
- Complexity of procedures;
- Differences in levels of decision-making and a lack of coordination or coherency between the national/regional/local levels;
- Lack of co-ordination and co-operation between institutions and departments involved in social protection at all levels of society.

At the level of system management:

- Failure to establish management structures for the design and implementation phases of action programmes;
- Failure to delegate powers and responsibilities on the part of institutions or administrative services implementing action programmes in the social protection sphere.

In a number of situations, all or some of these obstacles make access to rights particularly difficult or even a non-starter. Furthermore, the geography of states (regions) very often plays a considerable role in terms of obstacles and barriers, either because of distances between towns, topography or climatic conditions.

Recommendations

a) Strengthen partnership and participation of individuals and NGOs.

 Partnership should be stepped up between social protection bodies, social services, NGOs, social partners, etc. These partnerships should include direct involvement and expression for individuals in order to promote participation and autonomy on their part.

b) Ensure participation of people with disabilities in the implementation of policies and initiatives concerning them.

This implies that the NGOs are recognised in legal terms and their activity is encouraged and supported. However, as NGOs are not there to make up for the shortcomings of social bodies

177

and services, their involvement in framing and assessing policies and measures aimed at people with disabilities should be conceived for the purpose of improving and guaranteeing access to social protection for people with disabilities.

c) Reinforce compensatory machinery and programmes.

In the sphere of social protection policies and systems, this means reinforcing compensatory machinery and programmes concerning employment, public health, education, housing, transport etc. and ensuring the establishment of a universal "safe" income differentiated from complementary benefits (technical assistance, human assistance) compensating for disability.

2. Access to housing, built environment, town life and transport

The following obstacles may be identified:

The patent inadequacy of European standards governing accessibility of the built environment (hotels, public buildings etc) and the lack of means of ensuring that they are complied with are factors that exacerbate the exclusion of people with disabilities from life in society and perpetuate or even build on the obstacles faced by those individuals.

Recommendations

a) Enable each individual to live independently

Access to rented, private, co-operative or public-sector housing for people with disabilities, at an affordable price, should be fostered through the introduction *inter alia* of measures enabling each individual to live independently in ordinary housing integrated in the town environment. To achieve this aim, all housing built should be accessible and adaptable, and grants and/or tax relief should be provided so that existing housing is adapted.

b) Broaden the range of housing possibilities

A broad spectrum of housing possibilities should also be made available, ranging from ordinary specially fitted housing, with therapeutic or social assistance where needed,

178

through semi-community accommodation to accommodation in institutional facilities. Alongside these housing possibilities alternative forms of domestic cohabitation should be available, such as short-stay centres or placement families.

c) In the sphere of housing, buildings and access to town and transport, it is necessary to:

- be able to live in the environment of one's choice. Measures should be introduced, in legislative form, enabling those so wishing to live in the environment of their choice

- cease planning large accommodation units. The planning of large accommodation units (with or without integrated medical care) should be dropped.

- implement standards of accessibility common to the member states. Minimum standards of accessibility applicable to all states should be devised and implemented in order to build a continent-wide area accessible to all.

- build a continent-wide area accessible to all. The creation of a Europe-wide area accessible to all citizens, regardless of their disability, age etc. must enable every individual to lead an independent life.

This requires *inter alia* the introduction of shared minimum standards of accessibility, including in the field of technologies and communication, in order to eliminate all forms of segregation of and discrimination against people with disabilities and to ensure, on an equal footing:

- full access to urban infrastructures (including signposting and communication promoting free access to services);

- full access to common consumer-oriented industrial products, vehicles and transport services;

- full access to housing in accordance with rules on accessibility.

The principle of design for all makes it possible to promote independent life, through the application of integrative technologies to built environments, public areas and services, communication systems or housing, and to cut down the obstacles and barriers in all situations and places.

3. Access to health systems and medical care for people with disabilities and dependent people with disabilities

Obstacles blocking access to health systems and medical care:

- Inadequate co-ordination of services hampers co-operation between care, re-education or rehabilitation services, particularly since several years are often necessary to properly diagnose an impairment;

- All too often, staff (carers and paramedics) do not make proper allowance for the fact that people with disabilities have the same rights as any other patient;

- The failure to respect the rights of people with disabilities is at the root of worsening relations between the individual and the care staff.

In many cases health care system coverage focuses essentially on the medical aspect alone and neglects the social and environmental aspects.

Recommendations

a) Set up a coherent global policy in the health field.

A coherent global policy in the health field aimed at obviating any kind of stigmatisation should be based on a completely fair system guaranteeing access to care regardless of a person's financial resources.

b) Consider the impact of other policies on health policy.

A key factor in social coherence is consideration of the impact of other policies, systems and services (transport, food, housing, employment, education, environment, communication etc.) on health policy.

The aim of any health policy should be to offer universal cover by making services truly accessible to all, on the basis of:

- human rights and patients' rights;
- human dignity, social cohesion;
- democracy, equity, solidarity;
- equal opportunities between women and men;

180

– participation and freedom of choice balanced with the obligation to help every individual to consolidate their health.

c) Obtain consent for any act or treatment.

Information in the sphere of care should include the obligation to obtain the consent of individuals for any act or treatment. Furthermore, in accordance with the provisions of the Convention for the protection of human rights and fundamental freedoms, people with disabilities should be entitled to refuse treatment and not be subjected to forced admission to a specialised establishment.

d) Give priority to maintaining people with disabilities at home.

Maintaining people with disabilities in the home environment should be a priority of public policies and initiatives. This requires the service offer to be geared to facilitating home life for people with disabilities and their helper.

e) Seek prevention through health promotion.

Preventing incapacities and disabilities needs health promotion strategies at all levels of society, from citizens in their specific contexts (school, workplace, healthcare department etc.) to local and national authorities. The promotion of incapacity and disability prevention and health must be an integral part of all public policies.

f) Eliminate all forms of segregation and discrimination.

And pursue this objective in respect of all people with disabilities by ensuring access to health and medical care enabling them, on an equal footing, to benefit from high-quality medical and re-education services and lead a dignified life.

4. Access to educative activities, schooling and higher education

The most commonly encountered obstacles to access to educative activities and schooling for children with disabilities include:

– The lack of training for teachers in dealing with and educating children with disabilities;

181

- A degree of access to school buildings and facilities that does not allow children with disabilities to live like other children in the school;
- A lack of tailored programmes adapted to the children's pace of learning.

For young adults reaching university level, the obstacles in the higher education sphere concern:

- The organisation of universities, which are ill-prepared to take students with disabilities;
- No or inadequate building access leaving some students with disabilities unable to reach the lecture rooms or other facilities;
- Numerous teaching staff - even more than in schools - who are ignorant with regard to disability, inadequate financial resources of students with disabilities.

The following lines of action have been recommended to overcome these obstacles. Like the recommendations set out in the report on "Access to social rights for people with disabilities in Europe", they must take due account in their application of the differences in culture and development between states.

In the educative activities and schooling sphere, the following recommendations could be made:

a) Implement a personalised educative and pedagogical project.

Whatever the structure providing educative activities or schooling, it should commit itself to a personalised pedagogical, educative and, where necessary, therapeutic project tailored to the needs, possibilities and wishes of the child or young adult. The family should be involved, as far as necessary, in devising, implementing, monitoring and assessing that personalised project.

b) Give priority to mainstream educative and schooling arrangements.

Educative activity and schooling within the general school system must be preferred to specialised facilities since shared learning situations foster mutual understanding and ultimately make it possible to reshape society's views on disabilities.

c) Ensure proper linkage between the systems of schooling, vocational training and higher education.

For the acquisitions of children and young adults with disabilities in the school system to become permanent, there must be proper linkage between school education, vocational training, higher education and employment, throughout the educational process.

Recommendations in the sphere of higher education are to:

a) Promote equal opportunities in the sphere of higher education.

Provisions and measures aimed at providing access to higher education for all citizens can be fulfilled only if there are truly equal opportunities for all.

b) Cut down financial obstacles.

In order to cut down financial obstacles to access to higher education, funding in the form of study grants should recognise the additional needs of students with disabilities.

In more general terms:

In the sphere of educative activities, schooling and higher education, it is vital to give people with disabilities access to mainstream teaching and learning facilities.

c) Include the issue of disability in teacher training.

The issue of disability should be a compulsory part of teacher training programmes.

d) Encourage the use of new technologies.

The use of new technologies, techniques and distance teaching methods should be encouraged, together with gateways between mainstream education systems and specialised systems.

183

5. Access to employment and vocational training

Numerous obstacles in the employment sphere

People with disabilities encounter numerous obstacles in this sphere, linked to factors such as:

– age, sex;

– level of training and qualifications;

– accessibility of places of work and training.

In terms of employment:

– A lack of flexible working hours and adjustments in working time;

– A lack of employment policy making it possible to reconcile family life and professional responsibilities;

– Reluctance to invest in adaptations (accessibility, technology etc) facilitating employment of people with disabilities;

– The degree of dependency and age of an individual may be further obstacles to access to employment. It can happen that the parents and friends of people with disabilities over-protect them, and they may be discouraged from undertaking training or accepting a job as a result.

Obstacles encountered in the areas of careers guidance and vocational training include:

– A lack of coherent and integrated national policy in the sphere of education, vocational training and life-long learning;

– A lack of trainers, suitable training resources and local employers offering in situ training opportunities;

– Difficulty of access to education and training programmes corresponding to the individual's capacities.

Together these various obstacles mean that many people with disabilities are constrained to remain dependent on social benefits, simply because it is impossible for them to gain access, in normal conditions, to the labour market.

184

Recommendations

Several lines of action, which must take due account in their application of the differences in culture and development between states, are as follows:

a) Make life-long learning strategies operative.

Development of life-long learning strategies must be brought into play in all cases where an individual's disability does not constitute a serious obstacle to their professional integration.

b) Make training facilities and programmes available.

The use of general training systems should be the rule. General vocational training facilities and programmes must be made fully accessible to all categories of people with disabilities and involve all business sectors to broaden the range of vocational choices.

c) Co-ordinate ordinary and specialised placement services.

In the area of vocational training and employment there should be systematic coordination of ordinary and specialised placement and guidance services as well as gateways providing an easy return to social protection systems in the event of individuals losing their job.

d) Develop partnerships and social dialogue.

Finally, active policies geared to the employment of people with disabilities could not do without active partnership involving all the players in social dialogue: employer's organisations, trade unions and associations of people with disabilities. The latter must be able to participate in the drawing up of employment strategies and setting up of measures for providing vocational guidance and training for people with disabilities.

6. Participation in society and access to information

In the field of information, which is key to participation, several factors constitute real obstacles for people with disabilities, such as:

- A lack of widely available, clearly worded information on all the legislative measures (grants, benefits, technical assistance, rights etc.) and active measures (schooling, employment, training, higher education etc.) from which people with disabilities may benefit;

- People with disabilities all too often find themselves in situations where the information they need is not accessible (unsuitable medium, complexity of messages etc.). This is particularly the case for individuals with a visual, hearing or mental deficiency:

    i. in the area of culture and leisure (restaurants, leisure centres etc.),

    ii.in the area of essential services (gas, electricity etc.),

    iii. in the area of health (instructions for use of medicines required in braille, sickness prevention in sign language etc.),

    iv. in the area of political rights (voting rights, security, justice etc.).

A number of obstacles to participation in society reinforce stigmatisation and discrimination. Here too, there are several factors, including:

- situations where people with disabilities are excluded from fully fledged participation in society, caused by long-term unemployment;

- society's visions of disability still abounding with images of monstrosity when it is not a fear of possible contagion;

- the stigmatising and discriminatory attitude and behaviour of staff of public authorities responsible for receiving people with disabilities;

- the particular situation of women with disabilities who suffer from the same kind of discrimination as women in general in relation to men;

- the difficulty of people with disabilities in participating on an equal footing in the activities and management of political parties and civil society and in setting up organisations at local, regional or national level in order to contribute

186

to and influence political life at all levels and participate in decision-making affecting them.

Recommendations

Several lines of action, which must take due account in their application of the differences in culture and development between states, are as follows:

a) Develop integrated social policies.

Action plans should be implemented to promote access to new technologies, drawing on the principles of initiatives inspired by the "design for all" idea. These principles, combined with those developed by "coherent policies", can be key to the emergence of societies capable of reducing inequality.

b) Raising awareness of those responsible for the economic sector.

Those responsible for the economic sector, employment, education, health and rehabilitation should be made aware of the need to adapt society to people with disabilities and the solutions potentially offered by the new technologies.

c) Make information and communication systems accessible.

Generally speaking, given the social importance of full participation for people with disabilities, they must be given access, whenever necessary and tailored as far as possible to their needs, to the information and communication system as well as to the new technologies and services they require to gain enough independence to engage in various economic, social, cultural, sporting and recreational activities.

d) Develop the capacity for action of people with disabilities.

The capacity for action of people with disabilities should be developed by introducing measures and means (organisations, associations, human and financial resources) enabling them to influence legislation and institutional machinery and participate in the decision-making process concerning them.

e) Reinforce machinery for evaluating public policies.

187

Machinery for evaluating public integration and non-discrimination policies should be reinforced. These policies must be assessed and evaluated in terms of their impact on social cohesion, social exclusion and health.

7. Conclusion

To conclude, what makes society is not interaction between people and their material or human environment but standards that govern, regulate and organise that interaction. The concrete enactment of access to social rights in societies whose organisation is founded on the idea of a universal right to citizenship and respect for dignity, implies that each of us has legal personality and that every individual is recognised as having a fundamental identity as a human being. Where people with disabilities are concerned, human rights are to be seen not as an ideology but as a principle of action capable of configuring social reality.

How will the Council of Europe Action Plan and the UN Convention help persons with disabilities?

Mr Stefan TRÖMEL
European Disability Forum (EDF)

Abstract

We are seeing a real change in the way societies approach disability. A paradigm shift from a medical model to a human rights-based model. Two complementary initiatives (Council of Europe action plan and UN Convention) are currently in process, which could and should make a major contribution to this process of change. The UN Convention is a legally binding instrument, while the Council of Europe action plan is by its very nature "morally' and "politically" binding. The Council of Europe action plan needs to be coherent and consistent with the UN Convention. The overarching principles of both initiatives should be the same: equal opportunities, self determination, respect for the diversity among disabled people, full participation of disabled people in society, non discrimination. What could be the contributions of these two initiatives to ensure a better protection of the rights of persons with disabilities?

- The adoption of comprehensive anti-discrimination legislations, outlawing discrimination on the ground of disability in all areas of life, covering all human rights: civil, political, cultural, economic and social.
- The prohibition of any new barriers and a timeframe to eliminate existing barriers.
- The provision of positive action measures, including quality services to persons with disabilities, designed in co-operation with them and their organisations.
- An increased mainstreaming of disability in all policy areas.
- A structured dialogue between public authorities and organisations of persons with disabilities on all initiatives which might affect disabled people.
- Prohibition of forced interventions and forced institutionalisation on the ground of disability.
- Replacement of large residential institutions by community based services.
- A revision of mostly old fashioned guardianship laws and the substitution by a process of supported decision making, which will ensure that persons with disabilities are in control of their own lives.
- The recognition of sign language as an official language for deaf persons using sign language.

To ensure these outcomes, the process to finalise these two instruments needs to be done in close partnership with the representative organisations of disabled people.

NOTHING ABOUT DISABLED PEOPLE WITHOUT DISABLED PEOPLE!

Presentation

Dear ladies and gentlemen,

I would reword the title of the presentation and say that the question and challenge is: Will the Council of Europe Action Plan and the UN Convention promote the rights of disabled people?

As you know, both initiatives are still in process and the answer to the question will depend on the final content of both documents. We are seeing a real change in the way societies approach disability. A paradigm shift from a medical model to a human rights based model. From our point of view, the two initiatives (Council of Europe Action Plan and UN Convention) which are currently in process could and should make a major contribution to this process of change.

The still provisional title of the Council of Europe Action Plan is a good indication of this shift. It started to be called Council of Europe action plan on disability. Now, it seems agreed that the Action Plan will be called Action Plan to promote the rights and full participation of persons with disabilities. This is much more than just a change in the title; it is a real change in the approach. The focus has moved from disability as an object to disabled people as subjects.

The discussion both in New York (on the Convention) and in Strasbourg (on the Action Plan) related to prevention of disability has also been very enlightening. The European Disability Forum (EDF) has stated from the outset that prevention of disability has no place in a Convention on the rights of persons with disabilities and in an action plan to promote the rights of disabled people.

There are important similarities and also differences between the two instruments. Both instruments are comprehensive, that is, they seek to cover all areas of life of disabled people or, using human rights language, cover civil, political, economic, cultural and social rights. The main difference between these instruments is that while the UN Convention is a legally binding instrument, the Council of Europe Action Plan is by its

190

very nature "morally' and "politically" binding. While the adoption of the Council of Europe Action Plan will most likely happen before the negotiations on the UN Convention will have finalised, it is very important to ensure that the Council of Europe Action Plan is coherent and consistent with the UN Convention. The Council of Europe Action Plan will provide more details than the Convention, but the principles and the human rights-based approach of both documents should be the same.

EDF considers that the overarching principles of both initiatives should include the following: non-discrimination, equal opportunities, self determination, respect for disability as an element of human diversity, full participation of disabled people in society, and equality between women and men.

What could be the contributions of these two initiatives to ensure a better protection of the rights of persons with disabilities? It should lead to the adoption of comprehensive anti discrimination legislations, outlawing discrimination on the ground of disability in all areas of life.

Apart from protecting disabled people from direct and indirect discrimination, a central concept in the protection from discrimination and in obtaining real equal opportunities for disabled people is the provision of reasonable accommodation for those disabled people that so require. This concept recognizes the fact, that some disabled people require some form of support in order to be able to fully take part in employment, education, etc.

Another key element is full accessibility. Obtaining a barrier-free society should be an objective for both initiatives. This means preventing the creation of new barriers and the gradual elimination of existing barriers. Accessibility has to be understood in the widest possible meaning, covering the access needs of all disabled people. But - as the 2002 Madrid Declaration adopted by disability NGOs stated - to achieve the full inclusion of disabled people, positive action measures are also needed, including quality services for persons with disabilities, designed in co-operation with disabled people and their organisations.

The complete prohibition of forced interventions (medical and others) and forced institutionalisation on the ground of disability are also key objectives of the disability movement. Community-based services need to be established to allow a gradual closing down of all large residential institutions.

The replacement of the current models of guardianship, which take away from many disabled people the control over their lives, with models of supported decision-making, which ensure that disabled people maintain control over their lives.

The recognition of sign language as an official language for deaf persons using sign language and the recognition of Braille as the main literacy tool for blind people.

It is also very important that both initiatives give special attention to women with disabilities, children with disabilities and disabled people in need of a high level of support.

Both initiatives include an implementation and monitoring section. This is a vital element of both processes. If we don't ensure an adequate implementation and monitoring, the contribution of both instruments to a better protection of the rights of disabled people might be irrelevant. Monitoring needs to happen first at national level, but also at international level and NGOs of disabled people need to be able to take part in the process as the key stakeholder.

Also, both initiatives should contribute to an increase in the mainstreaming of disability in all policy areas. It is the responsibility of all areas and levels of decision making to take into account disabled people in the design and implementation of their policies.

This requires the establishment of a structured dialogue between public authorities and organisations of persons with disabilities on all initiatives which might affect disabled people. "Nothing about us without us" has been the slogan of EDF for many years and has also been the slogan used by all disability NGOs taking part in the UN Convention negotiations.

192

If we get all these things right, the answer to the question at the beginning of this presentation will be positive. To ensure this, the process to finalise these two instruments needs to be done in close partnership with the representative organisations of disabled people. Let's all work together to ensure this.

Thank you very much for your attention.

CONCLUSIONS AND CLOSING

Conclusions and the way forward

Mr Alexander VLADYCHENKO
Director General ad interim of Social Cohesion,
Council of Europe

Mrs Chairperson, Secretary of State, Ladies and Gentlemen, dear friends,

We are now at the end of a meeting of experts, and the crucial questions are:

"What have we learned from this conference?" and

"Where shall we go from here?"

1. We have learned what the issues are:

When we talk about disability, we talk about a considerable share of the population: although the WHO estimates that 10% of the population have a disability, this conference has shown that behind and around every disabled persons there is a family, so it is correct to say that disability probably affects 30 - 40 % of the population.

Far too many people with disabilities in general, and children with disabilities in particular, still live in institutions. The main problems in institutions are:

— higher than average mortality rates;

— malnutrition;

— overmedication;

— abuse of restraint;

— no rehabilitation;

– no way out.

The main obstacles to deinstitutionalisation are:

– resistance from institutions, from professionals, and from some parents or relatives who are unable or unsupported to face the challenge;

– widespread prejudice against people with disabilities amongst the population as a strong obstacle against living in the community, known as the NIMBY-phenomenon: "They may live in the community, but Not In My Back Yard!";

– lack of functioning models of community-based rehabilitation;

– lack of trained staff;

– lack of legislative framework.

One argument against deinstitutionalisation is that mainstream services cannot possibly obtain or provide the level of expertise found in special settings. The results are that:

– Disabled people are less well educated that the rest of the population;

– Disabled people participate less in working life;

– Households with disabled family members have lower income levels than other households;

– Disabled people frequently encounter financial difficulties;

– Disabled people live in poorer accommodation that the rest of the population.

In a nutshell: disabled people face a high risk of poverty, exclusion, marginalisation, ill-health, lack of education and vocational training, unemployment, abandonment, and institutionalisation.

2. We have learned what could be possible solutions

You discussed the dichotomy of inclusion as a means to an end (e.g. learn more) and inclusion as an end in itself, because the participation of all is a goal in itself. Examples of good practice from member states, as presented by delegates,

196

stressed that deinstitutionalisation should take place in stages. One step is to improve institutions by downsizing them, decentralising them, making them more home like and integrating them in the community. The other step, which should run in parallel, is to develop local, community-based services. The overarching aim, however, is to improve all services, inside and outside of institutions, through quality assurance. Another common position was that every intervention and service provision should be based on a sound assessment of the persons abilities, potential and specific requirements. The assessment should be multidisciplinary and shift from the deficit approach to the competency approach, which means to an assessment of abilities rather than disabilities. An individual plan should be established for every person. The services to be provided should be tailor-made and person-centred, defined on the basis of the individual needs. They should be user-driven, not system-driven.

Agreement was also reached on the fact that active and cooperative parents are a pre-requisite for any improvement in the situation. Consequently, parents need a co-ordinated support systems including:

– divorce prevention;
– competency building amongst families;
– respite services;
– personal assistant schemes;
– lifespan perspective.

Guiding principles must be the concept of the earliest possible intervention, and the participation of children and families in taking decisions that concern them.

3. The way forward: the need for action at European level

The United Nations dispose of excellent human rights instruments, in our context notably the Convention on the Rights of the Child. The UN Standard Rules on the equalisation of opportunities for people with disabilities have just celebrated their 10th anniversary. A UN convention to protect the human

197

rights and dignity of persons with disabilities is currently being drafted in New York. This new worldwide instrument is very much to be welcomed, but the questions are will it be targeted enough to protect the interests of disabled children and their families? And when will it be ready?

The Council of Europe also disposes of excellent human rights instruments, first and foremost the European Convention on Human Rights with the European Court of Human Rights here in Strasbourg to monitor is implementation, and the Human Rights Commissioner to promote awareness and understanding of that instrument. Then the revised European Social Charter with its Article 15 and its collective complaints procedure. And finally some softer instruments such as the Recommendation on a coherent policy for people with disabilities, Resolutions on vocational assessment or universal design, a revised Social Cohesion Strategy, and the forthcoming Council of Europe Disability Action Plan.

These instruments create case law and progressive obligations for states to take positive steps. In the meantime, however, we have to develop policies to protect the specific interests of children with disabilities and their families.

So where could we go from here? I have four proposals to make

No. 1. The results of the Conference will feed directly into the process of drafting the Council of Europe Disability Action Plan. The Chairman of the Drafting Group will have taken note of your comments and the next meeting of the Group is at the end of this month. And please let me add something about that forthcoming Council of Europe Disability Action Plan (which will be for the whole Organisation not only for 18 members of the Partial Agreement "Disability is a pan-European issue):

- it will promote the shift from the medical to the rights-based approach;

- it will be an integral and coherent instrument, complementary to the UN disability convention;

198

- it will, however, not be a legally binding instrument, but more of a political tool;

- its overarching principles will be equal opportunities, independent living, full citizenship and active participation in the life of the community;

- it will address issues such as non-discrimination, positive action, community-based, integrated services, mainstreaming, elimination of existing barriers, prevention of new barriers, awareness raising, and the promotion of access to social rights for all people with disabilities in Europe.

No. 2. As regards the UN disability convention, the Council of Europe will use the means which are at its disposal to promote the inclusion of the Conference results into the UN drafting process.

No. 3. The 3rd Council of Europe Summit of Heads of State and Government will take place on 16-17 May 2005 in Warsaw. It will define the future role of the Council of Europe in the international and European political landscape. The current draft declaration makes reference to social cohesion as one of the pillars of peace, justice and democracy in Europe. We must make sure that the social cohesion chapter will also include disability in general and children with disabilities and their families in particular. I count on your support in this matter.

No. 4. At pan-European level, I believe, we need specific Council of Europe recommendations and guidelines to promote community living for children with disabilities (deinstitutionalisation), to help families to take care of their disabled children at home in order to avoid institutionalisation. Those instruments should both be concrete and specific, but also flexible enough to be easily adaptable to all member states, taking into account their different backgrounds and circumstances. The instruments could be elaborated by a small multidisciplinary group of experts, consisting of experts from the Committee of the Rehabilitation and Integration of People with disabilities (CD-P-RR), the European Committee for Social Cohesion (CDCS), its subordinate body the Committee of experts on children and families (CS-EF), as well as the

199

Education Committee, and possibly others. Such co-operation between relevant steering committees would pool expertise, avoid overlap or duplication, and create synergy effects. The same group would also define the methodology to follow for initiating a targeted disability policy review and assistance pro-gramme (legislation and practice) in member states focused on a policy for deinstitutionalisation, community integration of children with disability and support to families. The activity should be carried out at the level of all Council of Europe member states. Reviews would be carried out in member states on a voluntary basis. The Group could also work out the financial basis of such a review programme, seeking not only voluntary contributions from countries but also from other sponsors (insurances, foundations, etc.). I offer to put a DG III inter-service Secretariat Task Force at the disposal of that Group of experts.

4. Closing

I would like to close by thanking through you, State Secretaries, the Norwegian authorities for having made this conference possible. By declaring disability issues as one of the priorities of the Norwegian Chairmanship of the Committee of Ministers, you have put this topic so high on the political agenda in Europe. You have thus provided the perfect follow-up to the European Year of People with Disabilities 2003 and the Council of Europe Malaga Ministerial Conference on disability, permitting us to keep momentum. Norway has always been at the forefront of developments in social policy in general and disability policy in particular, thus creating a more cohesive and inclusive society.

Ladies and gentlemen,

As the Viking Gods used to say: "Everyone has his use". That means that every person is a valuable member of society, it means every child matters. To me this seems a perfect motto for a cohesive, inclusive society. It is high time we put that into practice.

Closing

Mr Hans Olav SYVERSEN
Secretary of State
Ministry of Family and Children Affairs
Norway

Ladies and gentlemen, friends,

It has been a great pleasure for me to take part in this conference on behalf of the Norwegian Chairmanship of the Committee of Ministers of the Council of Europe. In these last two days we have been together here to discuss policies towards equality of opportunity for people with disabilities. The main focus has been to identify policies and good practice that protects and promotes the rights and dignity of children with disabilities, a society which allows them to fully participate. We have been presented to, and discussed, the European human rights framework for disability policies, and have particularly focused on one central theme in present day disability policy: deinstitutionalisation. And we have seen that these topics are reflected in the ongoing processes both in the UN international convention and in the Council of Europe Action Plan.

Deinstitutionalisation has also been the theme in workshop 1, because this is a major challenge – we all know that institutional thinking is alive in all European countries, even though some countries have stronger traditions for large institutions than others do. We have to have alternatives! Not just to shut down – we need adequate alternatives. In workshop 2 we have looked deeper into the lives of disabled children and their families. And again, we have focused on disabled children living with their families, not in institutions. The future of these children is fundamentally influenced by the attitudes that we all have towards disability. We want an inclusive society, and we must focus on all potentialities that the individual child has and concentrate on abilities rather than disabilities! I must say your statement, Miss Mangiafico, on yesterday's workshop, made a great impact on me.

201

The UN Convention on the Rights of the Child gives children with disabilities their own human rights. According to article 23 of the convention a mentally or physically disabled child should enjoy a full and decent life, in conditions which ensure dignity, promote self-reliance and facilitate the child's active participation in the community.

Most adults want to do what's best for the child. Still, adults often fail to ask children what they think is best for them. This summer, Norway hosted the 8th International Congress on Including Children with Disabilities in the Community. The success of the conference was due to the fact that young people themselves were active participants at various stages of the planning process and in drawing up the declaration. Young people, some of them with severe disabilities, were eloquent speakers in the plenary sessions as well as in work-shops, and in meeting points. The young people who met at the conference still have follow-up meetings on their Internet website. This once again proves the importance of contributions by children and adolescents in all issues related to their participation in society.

Sustainable policies for the family in all its forms are conductive to a safer environment and sound upbringing of children. I would like to use this opportunity to highlight one specific topic families often mention as a huge challenge in their everyday life: Children with reduced functional ability often require assistance from various parts of the public help system. They will need measures and services in several areas: Health services, medical help, physiological support, physiotherapy, technical aids, social services, special-education help, child day care services and school services, financial support schemes, transport, etc. This means that the families have to be in contact with several service systems. Families often experience that they themselves have to administer and coordinate the measures relating to the child. This takes time and resources and is often experienced as an extra burden on the families.

It is therefore of great importance to provide services to these families which are well co-ordinated and adapted to their needs, so that the families are made capable of caring for the child. Another very important consideration is that families, through the co-ordinated services, should have the opportunity to enjoy a social life outside the family, and should be given the opportunity to take part in working life.

In this context I would like to mention two interesting measures we find encouraging in Norway, and in which my Ministry supports financially and increasingly so for 2005. The first one is help and support to families, also families with children with reduced functional ability, through a parent volunteer connected to the Home-Start programme. I suppose a lot of you know this family support me, developed in the United Kingdom, and used all over the world. It can be of great support to families in periods when they could "need a hand".

The next measure was presented in workshop 2, so I know some of you have learned a lot about it already. But we are quite proud of it, so I take this opportunity to mention it once more: It started as a project baptised "What about us?" aiming at enhancing communication, strengthening relationships and preventing divorce in families with disabled children. One goal was also to establish and improve the co-operation with other institutions (hospitals, rehabilitation services, educational services etc.). Therefore we want this to be a permanent programme. Next step: single parents with children with disabilities. We know that there is a heavy demand for these workshops.

One important priority during the Norwegian Chairmanship of the Committee of Ministers of the Council of Europe has been to reinforce human rights and legal co-operation as mentioned by our ambassador last night. The discussions the last two days have been an important part of our Chairmanship programme. It is also an important part of the work of the ongoing processes within the Council of Europe on the

203

protection and promotion of the rights and dignity of people with disabilities.

During these past two days we have exchanged knowledge and ideas about how to dismantle disabling barriers. I believe that we have all learned something of importance that will enable us to strengthen the human rights for children, as well as grown-ups, with disability. As said in the opening speech by State Secretary Kristin Ravnanger, the challenge now is to transform our knowledge and intentions into legal and political documents, both national and international, and thereby create our road maps for an inclusive Europe. With reference to what Mr. Vladychenko has just said about the need for action: Norway supports and has great expectations to further work with Council of Europe Disability Action Plan. The idea of setting up a small multidisciplinary group seems to be relevant for the following up work, and Norway we will see in what way we can assist you in this matter.

We want children with disabilities to enjoy the same rights as anybody else. Still, many children with disabilities feel humble and not entitled to the same rights as others. In a Norwegian report to the UN Special Session on Children in 2002, young people with disabilities were quoted. A young girl with CP says: "It's like they think we've got nothing important to do. They think we should be happy as long as we're picked up and taken to some place at a certain time. We're not supposed to complain." Responding to the feeling of being looked at, another girl, 14 years, says: "When people stare, I ask if there's anything I can do for them. They get so embarrassed."

This is the last of many important events Norway has hosted during its chairmanship of the Committee of Ministers. Tomorrow our chairmanship will come to its end, and Poland will embark on six months of hard work. I am confident that Poland will follow the line of continuation and lead the work both dynamically and effectively. As mentioned by Mr. Vladychenko and Mr. Reinertsen, it's important that the subjects we have discussed on this conference can be a part of

204

the 3rd summit of the Council of Europe in Warsaw next May. I encourage all of you to work through your channels to promote such an agenda.

I would like to thank the Council of Europe and the Secretariat who have done all in their power to make this conference a success; you have done a splendid job! That goes for the interpreters as well.

Thank you for your active participation and attention!

PROGRAMME

Scope and objectives

During the European Year of People with Disabilities 2003, European Ministers reaffirmed their commitment to securing human rights and fundamental freedoms for everyone without any discrimination or distinction on disability or any other ground. (Second European Conference of Ministers responsible for integration policies for people with disabilities, Malaga, Spain, 7-8 May 2003, entitled "Improving the quality of life for persons with disabilities").

The Ministers undertook to work towards mainstreaming equality of opportunity for people with disabilities throughout all policy areas. To fully realise this goal they recommended the elaboration of a Council of Europe Action plan for people with disabilities. The Council of Europe would in this way play an active part in the UN work on an international convention on the human rights of persons with disabilities. The drafting of both the Council of Europe Disability Action Plan and the UN Draft Disability Convention is well underway and co-operation has been established.

All children are our future, including children with disabilities.

The Council of Europe and the Norwegian chairmanship of the Council of Europe have organised this conference to discuss policies towards this group of children. The aim is to identify policies and good practice to create a society that protects and promotes the rights and dignity of children with disabilities and allows them to fully participate in it.

The Conference will stress the need for the development of a new multidisciplinary approach to replace the traditional

207

medicalised model in order to take account of the multiplicity of the rights and needs of persons with disabilities. This was the thrust of the political message of the Malaga Ministerial Conference.

The programme and main topics of the conference include a presentation of the Council of Europe draft Action Plan on Disability as a means to promoting such rights. In doing so the Conference will also promote the United Nations Convention for persons with disabilities currently being drafted and to which the Council of Europe contributes as observer. This Draft Convention follows the same approach as the Council of Europe draft Disability Action Plan. The Conference will thus act as a regional platform for spreading this new universal philosophy.

The cross-cutting issue of children will be addressed in two working sessions; one on the challenges of deinstitionalisation, the other on the issue of children with disabilities and their families. Here again what is called for is a reform of the current medical model in favour of a multidisciplinary approach through the assessment of the developmental potential of children, namely ability as opposed to disability. Such a process requires both full participation of the child and family and strong interagency co-operation.

Key questions to be addressed will be:

– How do Council of Europe instruments protect and promote the human rights of people with disabilities?

– How can the Council of Europe Action Plan on Disability help to implement the rights of disabled children and their families?

– How can we encourage and enable parents with disabled children to take care of them at home? Who can give them necessary support? (Examples of good practice)

– How should inter-agency co-operation be organised so that it operates in the best interest of disabled children and their families? (Examples of good practice)

**Conference on Human Rights – Disability – Children
Towards international instruments for disability rights –
the special case of disabled children,
Council of Europe, Strasbourg,
8 - 9 November 2004**

This Conference is organised by Directorate General of Social Cohesion, Council of Europe in co-operation with the Norwegian Presidency of the Committee of Ministers

Chairperson

Ms Kristin RAVNANGER
Secretary of State
Ministry of Labour and Social

Vice - Chairperson

Mr Christian KIELLAND
Senior Adviser
Ministry of Labour and Social Affairs, Norway

General Rapporteur

Professor Hilary BROWN
Professor of Social Care
Canterbury Christ Church University College,
United Kingdom

Venue

Council of Europe
Palais de l'Europe, Room 9 (2nd floor)
Avenue de l'Europe
F-67000 STRASBOURG, France

Languages

English and French

Fees

No registration fees charged

209

Contact

Ms Katie STEPHENS
Directorate General III – Social Cohesion
Council of Europe
F-67075 Strasbourg
Fax: +33 3 88 41 27 32
E-mail: katie.stephens@coe.int
Internet: www.coe.int/soc-sp

8 November 2004

08h00 – 09h30   Registration of participants

Plenary Session I: Opening

09h30 – 09h40   Welcome Address
                   Mr Terry DAVIS
                   Secretary General, Council of Europe

09h40 – 09h55   Opening speech
                   Ms Kristin RAVNANGER
                   Secretary of State
                   Ministry of Labour and Social Affairs
                   Norway

Plenary Session II: Human Rights framework

09h55 – 10h10   The Council of Europe and the protec-
                   tion and promotion of the human rights
                   of people with disabilities
                   Mr Manuel LEZERTUA
                   Director
                   Office of the Human Rights
                   Commissioner
                   Council of Europe

10h10 – 10h25   The role of the European Court of
                   Human Rights in the protection of the
                   rights and dignity of people with
                   disabilities
                   Mr Loukis LOUCAIDES, Cyprus,
                   Judge
                   European Court of Human Rights

210

10h25 – 10h40	The rights of persons with disabilities under the European Social Charter Mr Regis BRILLAT Head of the Social Charter Secretariat Directorate General of Human Rights Council of Europe
10h40 – 11h00	General discussion
11h00 – 11h30	Coffee Break

Plenary Session III: Introduction to the Themes

11h30 – 11h50	The draft UN comprehensive and integral international convention on the protection and promotion of the rights and dignity of persons with disabilities Mr Arnt HOLTE Chairman of the Norwegian Federation of Organisations of Disabled People (FFO), Member of the Norwegian delegation to the UN Ad Hoc Committee
11h50 – 12h10	Comments on the draft UN disability convention Mr Carlos SALAZAR Mexico, Permanent Observer to the Council of Europe
12h10 – 12h40	The draft Council of Europe Disability Action Plan Mr J. Th. SLUITER Chairman of the Council of Europe Disability Action Plan Drafting Group Senior Policy Adviser Ministry of Health, Welfare and Sport, The Netherlands
12h40 – 13h00	General discussion
13h00 – 14h30	Lunch

Parallel Workshops: Workshop 1: Deinstitutionalisation

Chair:	Mr Christian KIELLAND, Senior Adviser Ministry of Labour and Social Affairs, Norway
Rapporteur:	Ms Ellinor SUNDSETH, Director, State Council on Disability, Norway
14h30 – 15h20	Challenges of deinstitutionalisation Professor Jan TØSSEBRO Department of Social Work and Health Science, Norwegian University of Science and Technology
15h20 – 15h40	From Institutions to Inclusion Ms Diana HOOVER Executive Director Mental Disability Advocacy Centre (MDAC), Budapest, Hungary
15h40 – 16h00	Challenging Human Rights Violations of People with Disabilities Ms Bardhylka KOSPIRI Advocacy Group Coordinator Albanian Disability Rights Foundation
16h00 – 16h30	Coffee break
16h30 – 18h00	General discussion

Parallel Workshops: Workshop 2: Disabled children and their families

Chair :	Mr Helmut HEINEN (Belgium), Director, Office for people with disabilities German-speaking Community of Belgium
Rapporteur:	Mr Hervé FACCHINI, Trainer, Association – Information – Research, France

212

14h30 – 14h50	The Council of Europe's Revised Strategy for Social Cohesion in relation to the integration of children with disabilities Ms Marie-Cécile VADEAU-DUCHER Chairperson of the European Committee for Social Cohesion (CDCS) Ministry of Employment, Work and Social Cohesion, France
14h50 – 15h20	Assessing the potentialities of children with disabilities Ms Aase Frostad FASTING Specialist in clinical psychology/ neuropsychology Huseby National Resource Centre for Visual Impairment, Norway
15h20 – 16h00	Challenges for families taking care of disabled children Mr Berger HAREIDE Deputy Director General Directorate of Children, Youth and Family Affairs, Norway
16h00 – 16h30	Coffee break
16h30 – 16h50	The Parents' Perspective Ms Marchita MANGIAFICO Parent Advocate Malta
16h50 – 18h00	General discussion
18h15	Reception Restaurant Bleu

9 Novembre 2004

Plenary Session IV: Synthesis

09h00 – 09h20   Report of Workshop 1:
Deinstitutionalisation
Ms Ellinor SUNDSETH
Director
State Council on Disability, Norway
Rapporteur of Workshop 1

09h20 – 09h40   Report of Workshop 2:
Disabled children and their families
Mr Hervé FACCHINI
Psychomotrician
Association Information Research (AIR),
France
Rapporteur of Workshop 2

09h40 – 10h00   General discussion

10h00 – 10h20   Some recommendations for the Council
of Europe Disability Action Plan
Mr Marc MAUDINET
Director
National Centre for Studies and
Research on Disability and Social Misfit
(CTNRHI), Paris, France

10h20 – 10h40   How will the COE Action Plan and the
UN Convention help persons with
disabilities?
Mr Stefan TRÖMEL
European Disability Forum (EDF)

10h40 – 11h10   Coffee Break

11h10 – 11h40   How should the items discussed at the
conference be reflected in the Council of
Europe Disability Action Plan?

Plenary Session V: Conclusions and closing

11h40 – 11h50	Conclusions and the way forward Mr Alexander VLADYCHENKO Director General ad interim Directorate General of Social Cohesion, Council of Europe
11h50 – 12h00	Closing Mr Hans Olav SYVERSEN Secretary of State Ministry of Family and Children Affairs, Norway

LIST OF PARTICIPANTS

Etats membres

Albania

Ms Bardhylka KOSPIRI
Advocacy Group Coordinator
Albanian Disability Rights Foundation
Rr Mujo Ulqinaku, 26
AL-Tirana
Tel. +355 42 69 426
    +355 42 66 892
Fax. +355 42 39 991
E-mail: adrf@icc.al.eu.org

Mr Aleksander KOSPIRI
Personal assistant to Mrs Bardhylka KOSPIRI

Austria

Mr Robert BECHINA
Civil Servant IV/A/7
Ministry of Social Security, Generations and Consumer Protection
Stubenring 1
A-1010 Wien
Tel. +43 1 71 100-6321
E-mail: robert.bechina@bmsg.gv.at

Azerbaijan

Mr Gunesh RUS-TAMZADEH
Deputy to the Permanent Representative

Permanent Representation of Azerbaijan to the Council of
Europe
2, rue Westercamp
F-67000 Strasbourg
Tel. +33 3 90 22 20 90
Fax. +33 3 90 22 20 99
E-mail: azrepcoe@wanadoo.fr

Belgium

Mr Helmut HEINEN
Geschäftsführender Direktor
Office for Persons with Disabilities, German-speaking
Community of Belgium
Aachenerstrasse 69-71
B-4780 ST. Vith
Tel. +32 80 22 91 11
Fax. +32 80 22 90 98
E-mail: dpb@euregio.net
Web site: http://www.dpb.be

Mme Catherine MOLLEMAN
Research Department
Vlaams Fonds voor Sociale Integratie
van Personen met een Handicap
Sterrenkundelaan 30
B-1210 Bruxelles
Tel. +32 2 225 86 30
Fax. +32 2 225 84 05
E-Mail: catherine.molleman@vlafo.be

Mr Dirk MOMBAERTS
Directeur Service Le Kangourou
Dienst vroegtijdige thuisbegeleiding "De Kangoeroe" vzw
Brusselse Steenweg 7B
B-9090 Melle
Tel. +32 477 42 65 33
Fax. +32 9 323 53 53
E-mail: directie@dekangoeroe.be

Bulgaria

Ms Assia TCHOLASHKA
Head of International Relations Unit
Directorate for European Integration and International Relations
Ministry of Labour and Social Policy
2 Triaditza Street
BG-1051 Sofia
Tel. +359 2 980 22 43
Fax. +359 2 981 53 76
E-mail: atcholashka@mlsp.government.b

Ms Miglena IVANOVA
State Expert
Policy and Strategy for Social Protection Directorate
Ministry of Labour and Social Policy
2, Triaditza str.
BG-1051 Sofia
Tel. +359 28 11 96 44
Fax. +359 29 87 01 34
E-mail: miglena_ivanova@abv.bg

Ms Ophelia KUNEVA
Chief Expert Social Inclusion of People with Disabilities
Ministry of Labour and Social Policy
2, Triaditza Street
BG-1051 Sofia
Tel. +359 88 835 06 71
E-mail: OFI@ABV.BG

Mr Dinko KANCHEV
Bulgarian Lawyers for Human Rights Foundation
49, Gurko St., entra A, fl 3
BG-1000 Sofia
E-mail: hrlawyer@blhr.org

Czech Republic

Mrs Stanislava MAKOVCOVÁ
Department for Conception of Social Health Policy
Ministry of Labour and Social Affairs

Na Pořičnim právu, 1
CZ-12801 Praha 2
Tel. +420 221 92 28 34
Fax. +420 221 92 20 03
E-mail: stanislava.makovcova@mpsv.cz

Ms Barbora KOLÁROVÁ
Ministry of Health
Palackého Nám, 4
CZ-12800 Praha 2
Tel. +420 224 97 21 98
Fax. +420 224 91 60 01
E-mail: Barbora.Kolarova@mzcr.cz

Denmark

Mrs Signe HØJSTEEN
Advisor Officer Education
The Danish Council of Organisations of Disabled People
Kløverprisvej 10
DK-2650 Hvidovre
Tel. +45 36 38 85 30
E-mail: sih@handicap.dk

Estonia

Ms Piret KOKK
Chief Specialist of the Social Welfare Department
Ministry of Social Affairs
Gonsiori 29
EST-15027 Tallinn
Tel. +372 626 92 23
Fax. +372 699 22 09
E-mail: piret.kokk@sm.ee

Mr Tarmo KURVES
Chief Specialist of the Social Welfare Department
Ministry of Social Affairs
Gonsiori 29
EST-15027 Tallinn
Tel. +372 626 92 24

Fax. +372 699 22 09
E-mail: tarmo.kurves@sm.ee

Finland

Ms Päivi KOVANEN
Senior Research Associate
Department of Special Education
University of Jyväskyla
P.O.BOX 35
FIN-40014 Jyväskylän Yliopisto
Tel. +358 14 26 01 649
Fax. +358 14 26 01 621
E-mail: paivi.kovanen@edu.juu.fi

France

Mme Marie-Cécile VADEAU-DUCHER
Chargée des relations avec le Conseil de l'Europe
Ministère de la Santé, de la Famille et des Personnes Handicapées
8 av. de Ségur
F-75007 Paris
Tel. +33 1 40 56 73 70
Fax. +33 1 40 56 47 72
Mobile phone +33 6 86 93 63 78
E-mail: marie-cecile.vadeau-ducher@sante.gouv.fr

Mr Marc MAUDINET
Directeur du Centre Technique National d'Etudes et de Recherches sur les Handicaps et les Inadaptions
236 bis rue de Tolbiac
F-75013 Paris
Tel. +33 1 45 65 59 13
Fax. +33 1 45 65 44 94
E-mail: m.maudinet@ctnerhi.com.fr

M Dominique CHOPPIN
Administrateur APAH- Finances
4, Chemin Champ Notaire
F-21110 Tart le Haute

Tel. +33 6 09 45 44 73
Fax. +33 3 80 28 68 25
E-mail: dominique.choppin@dgi.finances.gouv.fr

Mr Hervé FACCHINI
Psychomotricien – Masseur – Kinésithérapeute
Association Information Recherche (AIR)
32 rue Victor Hugo
F-90850 Essert
Tel. +33 3 84 22 54 17
E-mail: herve-facchini@wanadoo.fr

Ms Sonia CARDONER
Présidente
Association Parentale d'Entraide aux Enfants atteints d'une
Infirmité Motrice Cérébrale (APEEIMC)
10 F, Avenue Achille Baumann
F-67400 Illkirch-Graffenstaden
Tel. +33 3 88 67 18 08
Fax. +33 3 88 67 18 08
E-mail: apeeimc@wanadoo.fr

Mr Michel OHRUH
Association Parentale d'Entraide aux Enfants atteints d'une
Infirmité Motrice Cérébrale (APEEIMC)
11 B rue de Wissembourg
F-67000 Strasbourg
Tel. +33 3 88 94 20 99
Fax. +33 3 88 94 26 21
E-mail: mmmmohruh@aol.com

Mlle Marie Irene BOUCHET-BRAUNSTEIN
Présidente
Collectif d'Intégration Scolaire (CISI)
21, avenue des Vosges
F-67000 Strasbourg
Tel. +33 3 88 36 04 95
Fax. +33 2 88 36 04 95
E-mail: mj-bouchet@moos.fr

Mlle Anaïs FRANÇAIS-MINOT
Consultante
4, rue Pascal
F-92120 Montrouge
Tel. +33 1 47 35 82 20
Tel. +33 6 03 85 689
Fax. +33 1 47 35 82 80
E-mail: anaisfrançais@yahoo.com

Georgia

Ms Elene MARCHILASHVILI
Deputy Director
International Law Department Rehabilitation (BAR)
Ministry of Foreign Affairs
4, Chitadze Street
GE-380018 Tbilisi
Tel. +995 39 28 46 24
Fax. +995 39 28 48 77
E-mail: elenamarchilashvili@yahoo.com

Germany

Prof Armin SOHNS
University of Applied Sciences Neubrandenburg
Am Schoftrieb 17
D-63589 Linsengericht
Tel. +49 60 51 47 58 10
Fax. +49 60 51 47 58 11
E-mail: sohns@fh-nb.de

Mrs Brigitte PERTL-WULF
Sonderschulrektorin
Schule für Geistigbehinderte
Mürelweg 3
D-77731 Willstätt
Tel. +49 78 52 97 860
Fax. +49 78 52 97 862
E-mail: poststelle@04111065.schule.bwi.de

Mr Christian-Ulrich SCHIRRMACHER
Teacher Special School
Integrationssport; Hoisbuetteler Sportverein
Brunsdorfer Weg 11c
D-22359 Hamburg
Tel. +49 40 604 77 21
Fax. +49 40 604 77 21
E-mail: ChristianSchirrmacher@web.de

Dr Otto H.L. MESSER
Lawyer
Former Deputy Director of the Directorate of Economic and
Social Affairs of the Council of Europe
Ludwig-Trick-Str. 27
D-77694 Kehl am Rhein
Tel. +49 78 51 80 70

Dr med. Elisabeth MESSER
Honorary President
Lebenshilfe für geistig Behinderte Kehl – Hanauerland
Ludwig-Trick-Str. 27
D-77694 Kehl am Rhein
Tel. +49 78 51 80 70

Mr Artur HESSLER
Senior Expert
Lebenshilfe Kehl
Anselm-Pflügerstr. 8
D-77694 Kehl-Kork
Tel. +49 78 51 32 52
E-mail: arturhessler@nergo.de

Ireland

Mr Jim McCAFFREY
Assistant Secretary
Disability Equality Unit
Department of Justice, Equality and Law Reform
Bishop's Square, Redmond's Hill
IRL-Dublin 2
Tel. +353 1 47 90 219

Fax. +353 1 47 90 296
E-mail: Jim X.McCaffrey/JUSTICE@JUSTICE

Iceland

Mr Jon Seamundur SIGURJONSSON
Head of Department of Social Security
Ministry for Health and Social Security
Vegmuli 3
IS-150 Reykjavik
Tel. +354 545 87 00
Fax. +354 551 91 65
E-mail: jon.seamundur@hts.stjr.is

Italy

Mrs Luisa BOSISIO
Italian National Council on Disability
Oiazza Giovine Italia, 7
I-00195 Roma
Tel. +39 6 37 35 00 87
Fax. +39 6 37 35 07 58
E-mail: lbfazzi@tiscali.it

Latvia

Mrs Daina PODZINA
Deputy Director
Social Service and Social Assistance Department
Ministry of Welfare
Skolas Str. 28
LV-1331 Riga
Tel. +371 70 21 668
Fax. +371 70 21 678
E-mail: daina.podzina@lm.gov.lv

Lithuania

Mrs Areta MIŠKINIENĖ
Deputy Head of the Children and Youth Division
Ministry of Social Security and Labour
A Vivuldio Street 11
LT-03610 Vilnius
Tel. +370 5 26 64 225

225

Fax. +370 5 26 64 209
E-mail: armiskiniene@socmin.lt

Luxembourg

Mr Jacques SCHLOESSER
Director
Service d'Intervension Precose Orthopédagogique
60 av. de la Faiencerie
L-1510 Luxembourg
Tel. +352 44 71 71
Fax. +352 44 71 81
E-mail: direction@sipo.lu

Malta

Ms Concetta Marchita MANGIAFICO
Vice President
National Parents Society for Persons with Disability
215, Marlboro, Misrah il-Barrieri
M-HMR 18 Santa Venera
Tel. +356 21 24 61 63
Fax. +356 79 09 17 19
E-mail: vancamil@onvol.net

Moldova

Ms Paulina TUDOS
Senior Specialist
International Relations Division
Ministry of of Labor and Social Protection
1, Vasile Alecsandri Str
MD-2009 Chisinau
Tel. +373 22 72 99 88
Fax. +373 22 73 87 13
E-mail: paulinatudos@hotmail.com

The Netherlands

Mr Hans J. SLUITER
Senior Adviser
Disabled Persons Policy Directorate

Ministry of Health, Welfare and Sports
Postbus 20350
Den Hague
NL-2500 EJ
Tel. +31 70 340 53 73
Fax. +31 70 340 5371
E-mail: jt.sluiter@minvws.n

Norway

Ms Kristin RAVNANGER (Chairperson)
Secretary of State
Ministry of Labour and Social Affairs
P.O.BOX 8032 Dep
N-0030 Oslo
Tel. +47 22 24 85 64
Fax. +47 22 24 27 68
E-mail: kristin.ravnanger@asd.dep.no

Mr Hans Olav SYVERSEN
Secretary of State
Ministry of Family and Children Affairs
P.O.BOX 8032 Dep
N-0030 Oslo
Tel. +47 22 24 25 59
Fax. +47 22 24 27 19
E-mail: hans.syversen@bfd.dep.no

Mr Torbjørn FRØYSNES
Ambassador Extraordinary and Plenipotentiary
Permanent Representative of Norway to the Council of
Europe
42, rue Schweighaeuser
F-67000 Strasbourg
Tel. +33 3 88 25 09 65
Fax. +33 3 88 25 10 44
E-mail: coe.strasbourg@mfa.no

Mr Olav REINERTSEN
Minister Counsellor
The Norwegian Mission to the Council of Europe

42, rue Schweighaeuser
F-67000 Strasbourg
Tel. +33 3 88 25 09 65
Fax. +33 3 88 25 10 44
E-mail: ore@mfa.no

Mr Christian Boe KIELLAND (Vice-Chairperson)
Conseiller Principal
Ministry of Labour and Social Affairs
P.O.BOX 8019 Dep
N-0030 Oslo
Tel. +47 22 24 85 64
Fax. +47 22 24 27 68
E-mail: christian.kielland@asd.dep.no

Mr Bjørn BREDESEN
Deputy Director General
Department Children and Youth
Ministry of Children and Family Affairs
P.O.BOX 8032 Dep
N-0030 Oslo
Tel. +47 22 24 25 59
Fax. +47 22 24 27 19
E-mail: bjorn.bredesen@bfd.dep.no

Mr Berger HAREIDE
Deputy Director General
Directorate of Children, Youth and Family Affairs
P.O.BOX 8113 Dep
N-0032 Oslo
Tel. +47 29 04 41 48
Fax. +47 29 04 40 01
E-mail: berger.hareide@bufdir.no

Ms Gerd Juel HOMSTVEDT
Ministry of Health and Care Service
P.O.BOX 8011 Dep.
N-0030 Oslo
Tel. +47 22 24 83 83
Fax. +47 22 24 27 68

Mobile. +47 97 54 25 11
E-mail: gjh@hod.dep.no

Ms Karin ZETLITZ
Ministry of Labour and Social Affairs
P.O.BOX 8019 Dep
N-0030 Oslo
Tel. +47 22 24 85 93
Fax. +47 22 24 27 68
E-mail: kaz@asd.dep.no

Ms Birthe HUNDVIN
Adviser
Department of Children and Youth Policy
Ministry of Children and Family Affairs
P.O.BOX 8036 Dep
N-0030 Oslo
Tel. +47 22 24 24 34
Fax. +47 22 24 17 19

Mr Terje AALIA
Embassy Secretary
The Norwegian Mission to the Council of Europe
42, rue Schweighaeuser
F-67000 Strasbourg
Tel. +33 3 88 25 09 65
Fax. +33 3 88 25 10 44
E-mail: teaa@mfa.no

Ms Ellinor Joan SUNDSETH
Director
The Norwegian State Council on Disability
P. O. BOX 7075 St. Olavs plass
N-0130 Oslo
Tel. +47 24 16 30 98
Mobile. +47 48 08 26 67
Fax. +47 24 16 30 04
E-mail: esu@shdir.no

Mr Arnt HOLTE
President
Federation of Organisations of Disabled People
Sandakerveien, 99
N-0054 Oslo
Tel. +47 23 21 50 38
Fax. +47 25 56 76 95
Mobile phone: +47 90 19 07 32
E-mail: aholte@ffo.no

Ms Pernille BRODAHL
Personal Assistant to Mr. HOLTE

Prof. Jan TØSSEBRO
Department of Social Work and Health Sciences
Norwegian University of Science & Technology
N-7491
Tel. +47 73 50 17 20
Fax. +47 73 50 18 85
E-mail: jan@svt.ntnu.no

Mrs Aase Frostad FASTING
Specialist Clinical Psychology / Neuropsychology
Huseby National Resource Centre for Visual Impairment
Statped
Gml. Hovsetervei 3
N-0768 Oslo
Tel. +47 22 02 96 71
Fax. +47 22 92 15 90
E-mail: aase.frostad.fasting@statped.no

Ms Kari STEINDAL
Senior Adviser
The National Autism Network of Norway
University of Oslo
P.O. BOX 1144 Blindern
N-0480 Oslo
Tel: +47 22 85 88 51
Tel. +47 91 14 47 67
Fax. +47 22 85 88 59
E-mail: k.s.steindal@isp.uio.no

Mr. Gunnar TVEITEN
Assistant Director General
Ministry of Employment and Social Affairs
Tel. +33 6 70 47 57 79
E-mail: tveisand@online.no

Poland

Ms Malgorzata KIELDUCKA
Adviser to the Ministry
Office of the Government Plenipotentiary for Disabled
People
Ministry of Social Policy
4 Galczynskiego str.
PL-00-362 Warszawa
Tel. +48 22 826 12 61 ext. 120
Fax. +48 22 826 51 46
E-mail: malgorzata.kielducka@mps.gov.pl

Romania

Ms Olga JORA
Director
Government of Romania National Authority for Persons with
Disabilities
Calea Victoriei 194 Sector 1
RO-71101 Bucharest
Tel. +40 72 671 12 35
Fax. +40 21 312 08 04
Mobile phone: +40 740 16 16 70
E-mail: jora_olga@hotmail.com

Mr Dumitru LEULESCU
Director
National Authority for Child Protection and Adoption
Ministry of Labour, Social Solidarity and Family
7, Magheru Boulevard
RO-Sector 1, Bucharest
Tel. +40 21 31 00 789
Fax. +40 21 31 27 474
E-mail: dumitru_leulescu@anpca.ro

Mrs Adina DRAGOTOIU
Counsellor
Ministry of Labour and Social Solidarity
Dem I. Dobrescu Street, Sector 1
RO-70000 Bucharest
Tel. +40 21 31 58 609
Fax. +40 21 31 21 317
E-mail: adinadragotoiu@mmssf.ro

Mr Nicu Sorin TURTUREA
Senior Adviser
National Authority for Child Protection and Adoption
Ministry of Labour, Social Solidarity and Family
7, Magheru Boulevard
RO-Sector 1, Bucharest
Tel. +40 21 31 00 789
Fax. +40 21 31 27 474
E-mail: nicu_sorin_turturea@anpca.ro

Russia

Alexander KLEPIKOV (apologised/excusé)
All-Russian Society of Disabled People
Udaltsova 11
RUS-Moscow 117415
Fax. +7 095 935 00 64
E-mail: id.voi@relcom.ru

Slovenia

Ms Aleksandra TABAJ
Senior Advisor
Section for People with Disability
Ministry of Labour, Family and Social Affairs
Kotnikova 5
SLO-1000 Ljubljana
Tel. +386 1 431 71 81
Fax. +386 1 232 19 48
E-mail: aleksandra.tabaj@gov.si

Spain

Ms Encarnacion BLANCO EGIDO
Asesora
Dirección General de Coordinación de Políticas Sectoriales
sobre la Discapacidad
Ministerio de Trabajo Y Asuntos Sociales
c/ Jose Abascal , 39
E-28071 Madrid
Tel. +34 91 36 38 171
E-mail: eblancoe@mtas.es

Sweden

Ms Kerstin JANSSON
Desk Officer
Ministry of Health and Social Affairs
S-10333 Stockholm
Tel. +46 8 40 53 207
Fax. +46 8 10 36 33
E-mail: kerstin.jansson@social.ministry.se

Turkey

Mr Ahmet KARAMERCAN
Adviser of Minister of Education
Foreign Affairs and Disability Children
Ministry of National Education
Milli Egitim Bakanligi, Bakanlik Müsaviri
Bakanlik Kati Bkanliklar
Ankara
Tel. +90 31 24 24 08 95/96
Mobile +90 53 37 67 58 78
Fax. +90 31 24 17 70 27
E-mail: akaramercan@meb.gov.tr

Mrs Aysegul YESILDAĞLAR
Head of the EU Coordination Dep
Ministry of Social Security and Labour
Inŏnŭ Bulvari 42
TR-06520 Emek- Ankara

Tel. +90 312 212 56 12
Fax. +90 312 212 11 48
E-mail: calisab@csgb.bov.tr

Ukraine

Mrs Valentyna PUTSOVA
Deputy Head of International Relations Department
Ministry of Labour and Social Policy
8/10 Esplanadna St
UA-01023 Kiev
Tel. +38 044 220 71 85
Fax. +38 044 220 90 28
E-mail: pvg@mlsp.gov.ua

United Kingdom

Dr. Peter WRIGHT
Medical Policy Advisor
Department of Work and Pensions
Room 632, The Adelphi building
1-11 John Adam Street
GB-London WC2N 6HT
Tel. +44 20 77 12 23 33
Fax. +44 20 77 12 23 30
E-mail: peter.wright@dwp.gsi.gov.uk

Ms Alison THOMPSON
SEN Framework & Transsition Team
Special Educational Needs & Disability Division
Department for Education and Skills
4D, Caxton House
6-12 Tothill Str
GB-London SW1H9NA
Tel. +44 207 273 5329
E-Mail: alison.thompson@dfes.gsi.gov.uk

Prof. Hilary BROWN (GENERAL RAPPORTEUR)
Professor of Social Care
Canterbury Christ Church University College
127 Stephens Road

Tunbridge Wells
GB-Kent TN3 OTG
Tel. +44 18 92 51 51 52
Fax. +44 18 92 54 03 54
E-mail: h.j.brown@salomons.org.uk

Ms Philippa RUSSEL (apologised/excusée)
Council for Disabled People
8, Wakley Street
GB-London EC IV 7 QE
Tel. +44 171 843 60 00
Fax. +44 171 278 95 12
E-mail: prussel@ncb.org.uk

Observer States

Holy See

Mgr. Vito RALLO
Observateur Permanent auprès du Conseil de l'Europe
2, rue de Nôtre
F-67000 Strasbourg
Tel. +33 3 88 35 02
E-mail: saint-diege-strg@wanadoo.fr

Mr Michel GYSS
Président
Association Personnes Handicapées GLAUBITZ
M.P. Saint-Siège
12 allée de Vignoble
F-67210 Obernai
Tel. +33 3 88 95 56 59
E-mail: michelgyss@bigfoot.fr

Japon

Mlle Etsuyo NISHIYAMA
Chargée de mission
Consultat Général du Japon
Tour Europe
20 Place des Halles

F-67000 Strasbourg
Tel. +333 88 52 85 16
Fax. +333 88 22 62 39
E-mail: etsuyo.nishiyama@dial.oleane.com

Mexico

Mr Carlos SALAZAR-DIEZ DE SOLLANO
Deputy Permanent Observer
Permanent Mission of Mexico to the Council of Europe
8, bd du Président Edwards
F-67000 Strasbourg
Tel. +33 3 88 24 26 81
Fax. +33 3 88 24 10 87
E-mail: csalazar@wanadoo.fr

Other Participants

International Non-Governmental Organisations

*Confédération des Organisations des Familles des
Handicapées de l'E.U. (COFACE)*

Mme Anna Maria COMITO
Présidente de COFACE – HANDICAP
Confederation des Organisations des Familles des Personnes
Handicapées de l'E.U.
Rue de Londres, 17
B-1000 Bruxelles
Tel. +32 2 511 41 79
Fax. +32 2 514 47 73
E-mail: a.comito@tin.it

*European Agency for Development in Special needs
Education*

Mr Jørgen GREVE
Director
European Agency for Development in Special Needs
Education
102 Teglgaardsparken

DK-5500 Middelfart
Tel. +45 64 41 00 20
Fax. +45 64 41 23 03
E-mail: jg@european-agency.org

Ms Axelle CHENEY
Project Assistant
European Agency for Development in Special Needs
Education
Avenue Palmerston 3
B-1000 Brussels
Tel. +32 22 80 33 58
Fax. +32 22 80 17 88
E-mail: axelle.cheney@european-agency.org

EU Monitoring and Advocacy Program (EUMAP)

Ms Katy NEGRIN
Program Officer
Open Society Institute
Nádor u. 11
H-1051 Budapest
Tel. +36 1 327 31 00 ext 2481
Fax. +36 1 327 31 01
E-mail: knegrin@osieurope.org

European Association for Service Providers for People with Disabilities (EASPD)

Ms Hilde DEKEYZER
Research and Development Officer
European Association of Service providers for People with
Disabilities (EASPD)
Oudergemlaan 63
B-1040 Brussesl
Tel. +32 2 282 46 11
Fax. +32 2 230 72 33
E-mail: hilde@easpd.org

European Disability Forum (EDF)/
Forum European des Personnes Handipées (FEPH)

M. Stefan TRÖMEL
European Disability Forum (EDF)
rue du Commerce 39-41
B-1000 Bruxelles
Tel. +32 2 282 46 00
Fax. +32 2 282 46 09
E-mail: stromel@fundaciononce.es

European Trade union Confederation (ETUC)

Mr Henri LOURDELLE
Conseiller
Conféderation Européenne des Syndicats (CES)
Boulevard du Roi Albert II
B-1210 Bruxellles
Tel. +32 2 224 04 50
Fax. +32 2 224 04 54
E-mail: hlourdel@etuc.org

Inclusion International

Mr Alvaro GARCIA
Legal Officer
Inclusion International
Chaussé d'Ixelles 29   393/32
B-1050 Bruxelles
Tel. +32 2 50 22 815
Fax. +32 2 50 28 010
E-mail: secretariat@inclusion-europe.org

Mental Disability Advocacy Center (MDAC)

Ms Diana HOOVER
Executive Director
Mental Disability Advocacy Centre (MDAC)
P. O. Box 263
H-1241 Budapest
Tel. +36 1 413 27 30

Fax. +36 1 413 27 39
E-mail: dhoover@mdac.info

Rehabilitation International (RI)

Dr. Ulrich GERKE
Referatsleiter Internationale Beziehungen
Rehabilitation International (RI)
c/o Bundesarbeitsgemeinschaft für Rehabilitation (BAR)
Walter-Kolb-Str 9-11
D-60594 Frankfurt am Main
Tel. +49 69 60 50 18-26
Fax. +49 69 60 50 18-29
E-mail: ulrich.gerke@bar-frankfurt.de

Council of Europe

Secretary General

Mr Terry DAVIS
Secretary General
Council of Europe
F-67075 Strasbourg
Tel. +33 3 88 41 20 51
Fax. +33 3 88 41 27 99
E-mail: terry.davis@coe.int

Private Office of the Secretary General

Mr Dmitri MARCHENKOV
Administrative Oficer
Council of Europe
F-67075 Strasbourg
Tel. +33 3 88 41 38 44
Fax. +33 3 88 41 27 99
E-mail: dmitri.marchenkov@coe.int

European Court of Human Rights

Mr Loukis LOUCAIDES
Judge in respect of Cyprus
European Court of Human Rights

F-67075 Strasbourg
Tel. +33 3 88 37 38 36
Fax. +33 3 88 41 27 30
E-mail: loukis.loucaides@ehr.coe.int

Office of the Commissioner for Human Rights

M. Manuel LEZERTUA
Director
Office of the Commissioner for Human Rights
Council of Europe
F-67075 Strasbourg
Tel. +33 3 88 41 21 25
Fax. +33 3 92 21 50 53
E-mail: manuel.lezertua@coe.int

Protocol

M. Muammer TOPALOGLU
Director of Protocol
Council of Europe
F-67075 Strasbourg
Tel. +33 3 88 41 21 37
Fax. +33 3 88 41 27 73
E-mail: muammer.topaloglu@coe.int

Directorate of Communication and Research

Press Division

M. Can FISEK
Attaché de Presse
Conseil de l'Europe
F-67075 Strasbourg
Tel. +33 3 88 41 30 41
Fax. +33 3 88 41 39 11
E-mail: can.fisek@coe.int

M. Alban BODINEAU
Photographe
Conseil de l'Europe
F-67075 Strasbourg

Tel. +33 3 90 21 52 76
Fax. +33 3 88 41 27 08
E-mail: alban.bodineau@coe.int

Directorate General II – Human Rights

M. Régis BRILLAT
Head of the Social Charter Secretariat
Directorate General II – Human Rights
Council of Europe
F-67075 Strasboug
Tel. +33 3 88 41 22 08
Fax. +33 3 88 41 37 00
E-Mail: regis.brillat@coe.int

Mme Niamh CASEY
Administrative Officer
Social Cherter Secretariat
Directorate General II – Human Rights
Council of Europe
F-67075 Strasboug
Tel. +33 3 88 41 39 35
Fax. +33 3 88 41 37 00
E-Mail: niamh.casey@coe.int

Council of Europe Staff Committee

M. Jean-Pierre RINGLER
Comité du Personnel du Conseil de l'Europe
Groupe pour l'insertion professionnelle
des personnes handicapées
12 rue de la Tanche
F-67000 Strasbourg
Fax. +33 3 88 41 89 02
E-mail: jp.ringler@noos.fr

Directorate General III – Social Cohesion

Conference Secretariat

M. Alexander VLADYCHENKO
Director General *ad interim* of Social Cohesion
Council of Europe
F-67075 Strasbourg

241

Tel. +33 3 88 41 21 78
Fax. +33 3 88 41 37 78
E-mail: alexander.vladychenko@coe.int

Department of Health and of the Partial Agreement in the Social and Public Health Field

Mme Vera BOLTHO
Head of Department
Department of Health and of the Partial Agreement in the
Social and Public Health Field
Council of Europe
F-67075 Strasbourg
Tel. +33 3 88 41 21 73
Fax. +33 3 88 41 27 32
E-mail vera.boltho@coe.int

Division of the Partial Agreement in the Social and Public Health Field

M. Thorsten AFFLERBACH
Head of Division *ad interim*
Council of Europe
F-67075 Strasbourg
Tel. +33 3 88 41 28 23
Fax. +33 3 88 41 27 32
E-mail: thorsten.afflerbach@coe.int

M. Laurent LINTERMANS
Administrative Officer
Council of Europe
F-67075 Strasbourg
Tel. +33 3 90 21 40 10
Fax. +33 3 88 41 27 26
E-mail: laurent.lintermans@coe.int

Mme Sheila BOULAJOUN
Principal Administrative Assistant
Council of Europe
F-67075 Strasbourg

Tel. +33 3 88 41 21 75
Fax. +33 3 88 41 27 26
E-mail: sheila.boulajoun@coe.int

Ms Muriel GRIMMEISSEN
Administrative Assistant
Council of Europe
F-67075 Strasbourg
Tel. +33 3 88 41 28 19
Fax. +33 3 88 41 37 78
E-mail: muriel.grimmeissen@coe.int

Ms Angamah RAMEN
Assistant
Council of Europe
F-67075 Strasbourg
Tel. +33 3 88 41 33 05
Fax. +33 3 88 41 27 26
E-mail: angamah.ramen@coe.int

Ms Katie STEPHENS
Assistant
Council of Europe
F-67075 Strasbourg
Tel. +33 3 88 41 39 84
Fax. +33 3 88 41 27 26
E-mail: katie.stephens@coe.int

Ms Déborah GRETENER
Assistant
Council of Europe
F-67075 Strasbourg
Tel. +33 3 90 21 44 25
Fax. +33 3 88 41 27 26
E-mail: deborah.gretener@coe.int

Mrs Gerda BULTINCK
Assistant
Council of Europe
F-67075 Strasbourg

Tel. +33 3 90 21 52 44
Fax. +33 3 88 41 27 26
E-mail: gerda.bultinck@coe.int

Social Policy Department

Mlle Irena KOWALCZYK-KEDZIORA
Administrator, Responsable for the Family and Child Sector
Council of Europe
F-67075 Strasbourg
Tel. +33 3 91 21 44 34
Fax. +33 3 88 41 37 65
E-mail: irena.kowalczyk@coe.int

Ms Sheila PIDL
Assistant
Council of Europe
F-67075 Strasbourg
Tel. +33 3 90 21 2159
Fax. +33 3 88 41 27 32
E-mail: sheila.pidl@coe.int

Other Participants from DGIII

M. Vladimir TCHERNEGA
Technical Assistance Programmes Advisor
Social Policy Department
Council of Europe
F-67075 Strasbourg
Tel. +33 3 90 21 45 68
Fax. +33 3 88 41 27 18
E-mail: vladimir.tchernega@coe.int

Mrs Mona SANDBAEK
Programme Advisor
Social Policy Department
Council of Europe
F-67075 Strasbourg
Tel. +33 3 90 21 52 52
E-mail: mona.sandbaek@coe.int

Directorate General of Administration and Logistics

Interpreters

Mme Monique PALMIER
Mme Josette YOESLE-BLANC
Mme Cynera JAFFREY
Mme Nadine KIEFFER

LIST OF PUBLICATIONS

I. Recommendations and Resolutions

Resolution ResAP (2001) 3

Towards full citizenship of persons with disabilities through inclusive new technologies, booklet version

Resolution ResAP (2001) 3

Towards full citizenship of persons with disabilities through inclusive new technologies
(http://cm.coe.int/stat/E/Public/2001/adopted_texts/resAP/2001xp3.htm)

Resolution ResAP (2001) 1

on the introduction of the principles of universal design into the curricula of all occupations working on the built environment, booklet version

Resolution ResAP (2001) 1

on the introduction of the principles of universal design into the curricula of all occupations working on the built environment
(http://cm.coe.int/ta/res/resAP/2001/2001xp1.htm)

Resolution ResAP (95) 3

on a Charter on the vocational assessment of people with disabilities, and Glossary, booklet version
ISBN 92-871-3346-8, € 7.62 / US $ 12

Resolution ResAP (95) 3

on a Charter on the vocational assessment of people with disabilities
(http://cm.coe.int/ta/res/resAP/1995/95xp3.htm)

Recommendation N° R (92) 6

on a coherent policy for people with disabilities, booklet version, ISBN 92-871-2147-8   ? 7.62 / US$ 12

Recommendation N° R (92) 6

on a coherent policy for people with disabilities
(http://cm.coe.int/ta/rec/1992/92r6.htm)[1]

AP (84) 3[2]

Coherent policy for the rehabilitation of disabled people

AP (81) 8*

Information systems on impaired, disabled and handicapped people

AP (81) 7*

Possibilities of leisure and sports activities, and holidays for disabled persons

AP (77) 8*

Adaptation of housing and surrounding areas to the needs of disabled persons

AP (77) 7*

"Enclaves" for disabled people

---

* Recommendations and Resolutions marked with an asterisk have been replaced by
1. Resolution AP (84) 3. Available in Albanian, Belgian, Bulgarian, Dutch, Czech, English, Finnish, French, Hungarian, German, Italian, Polish, Latvian, Russian, Portuguese, Romanian, Slovenian and Spanish.
2. Resolution AP (84) 3 has been replaced by Recommendation N° R (92) 6.

AP (76) 4*

Possibilities of leisure activities and holidays for the disabled

AP (76) 3*

Identification of disabled persons

AP (76) 2*

Services for those disabled people who need special conditions of employment

AP (74) 8*

Ways of facilitating access to and use of means of public transport by disabled people

AP (73) 1*

Place of retraining for exertion and of pre vocational retraining in the rehabilitation cycle

AP (72) 5*

Planning and equipment of buildings with a view to making them more accessible to the physically handicapped

AP (72) 4*

Specialised transport for legless persons and paraplegics as well as for other disabled persons who may be assimilated thereto on account of the nature and seriousness of their disability

AP (72) 3*

Rehabilitation of children suffering from dysmelic syndromes

AP (72) 2*

Use of an international symbol indicating special facilities for the disabled

AP (71) 2*

Rehabilitation of persons suffering from chronic evolutive polyarthritis

AP (70) 2*

Rehabilitation of those suffering from heart disease, either congenital or due to acute rheumatic fever (Bouillaud's disease)

AP (69) 4*

The training of personnel concerned with rehabilitation

AP (67) 2*

Manufacture and supply of prostheses

AP (67) 1*

Rehabilitation of old people receiving care at home and in homes for the aged

AP (66) 5*

Rehabilitation of persons suffering from speech defects

AP (66) 4*

Rehabilitation of deaf and partially deaf persons

AP (66) 3*

Rehabilitation of persons suffering from ankylosing spondylitis

AP (66) 1*

The abolition of customs duties levied on prostheses for disabled persons

AP (65) 1*

Sheltered employment

AP (63) 2*

Health education with regard to the rehabilitation of physically and mentally handicapped persons

250

AP (63) 1*

Rehabilitation of old people

AP (60) 2*

Rehabilitation of the disabled during employment

II. Publications

The status of sign languages in Europe (2005),
ISBN 92-871-5720-0, € 17 / US $ 26

Citizens not patients – developing innovative approaches to meet the needs of disabled people (2004) free

Community living for people with disabilities in need of a high level of support (2004) free

Legislation to counter disctrimination against persons with disabilities, 2nd edition (2003),
ISBN 92-871-5314-0, € 13 / US$ 20

Discrimination against women with disabilities (2003),
ISBN 92-871-5316-7, € 8 / US$ 12

Access to social rights for people with disabilities (2003),
ISBN 92-871-5328-0, € 8 / US$ 12

Rehabilitation and integration of people with disabilities: policy and legislation, 7th edition (2003),
ISBN 92-871-5123-7, € 30 / US$ 45

Safeguarding adults and children with disabilities against abuse (2002),
ISBN 92-871-4919-4, € 17 / US$ 26

The impact of new technologies on the quality of life of persons with disabilities (2002),
ISBN 92-871-5007-9, € 19 / US$ 29

Rehabilitation and integration of people with disabilities: policy and legislation, 6th edition, (2002),
ISBN 92-871-4827-9, € 23 / US $ 35

Assessing disability in Europe - similarities and differences (2002),
ISBN 92-871-4744-2, € 23 / US$ 35

Cochlear implants in deaf children (2001),
ISBN 92-871-4628-4, € 8 / US$ 12

Legislation to counter discrimination against persons with disabilities (2000),
ISBN 92-871-4422-2, € 10,67 / US$ 18

Employment strategies to promote equal opportunities for persons with disabilities on the labour market (2000), ISBN 92-871-4216-5 , € 9,15 / US$ 15

Proceedings of the International Workshop on the use and usefulness of the International classification of impairments, disabilities and handicaps (ICIDH), Strasbourg 25-26 March 1996, (1999),
ISBN 92-871-3867-2, € 12,96 / US$ 21

Literature review of the International classification of impairments, disabilities and handicaps (ICIDH) (1998),
ISBN 92-871-3660-2, € 10,67 / US$ 18

The use and usefulness of the International classification of impairments, disabilities and handicaps (ICIDH) in the maintenance of people with disabilities at home and in their communities (1998),
ISBN 92-871-3620-3, € 7,62 / US$ 12

Vocational training and rehabilitation of people with disabilities: a comparative analysis (1997),
ISBN 92-871-3475-8, € 9,15 / US$ 15

The use and usefulness of the International classification of impairments, disabilities and handicaps (ICIDH) for the education of children with impairments or disabilities (1997),
ISBN 92-871-3427-8, € 10,67 / US$ 18

Sheltered employment in five member states of the Council of Europe (1997),
ISBN 92-871-3325-5, € 9,15 / US$ 15

Framework for the qualitative and quantitative analysis of data on the ageing of people with disabilities (1997),
ISBN 92-871-3327-1, € 9,15 / US$ 15

Use of the International classification of impairments, disabilities and handicaps (ICIDH) in relation to the elderly (1997),
ISBN 92-871-3315-8, € 9,15 / US$ 15

The transition from sheltered to ordinary employment (1996),
ISBN 92-871-3144-9, € 7,62 / US$ 12

Use and usefulness of the ICIDH for health professions (nursing, physical therapy, speech therapy, occupational therapy, chiropody and orthoptics) (1996),
ISBN 92-871-3004-3, € 9,15 / US$ 15

Assessment of the evaluations of the application of the ICIDH to the various spheres of rehabilitation and integration of people with disabilities (1996),
ISBN 92-871-2940-1, € 7,62 / US$ 12

Use and usefulness of the ICIDH for policy and planning of public authorities (1995),
ISBN 92-871-2858-8, € 7,62 / US$ 12

Use of the International classification of impairments, disabilities and handicaps (ICIDH) in the assessment of vocational aptitudes of people with disabilities Part I - General Report (1993),
ISBN 92-871-2388-8 , € 9,15 / US$ 15

Use of the International classification of impairments, disabilities and handicaps (ICIDH) in the assessment of vocational aptitudes of people with disabilities Part II - Methods of Assessment and the Index of Characteristics (1993),
ISBN 92-871-2390-X, € 9,15 / US$ 15

Applications of the concept of handicap of the International classification of impairments, disabilities and handicaps (ICIDH) and its nomenclature (1993),
ISBN 92-871-2421-3, € 7,62 / US$ 15

Accessibility: principles and guidelines (1993),
ISBN 92-871-2260-1, € 9,15 / US$ 15

Use of the International classification of impairments, disabilities and handicaps (ICIDH) in the field of mental retardation (1993), ISBN 92-871-2337-3, € 7,62 / US$ 12

Legislation on the rehabilitation of people with disabilities (1993), 5th edition,
ISBN 92-871-2316-0, € 14,48 / US$ 25

Use of the international classification of impairments, disabilities and handicaps (ICIDH) in the assessment of technical aids (1992),
ISBN 92-871-2137-0, € 7,62 / US$ 12

Training of staff, other than health care staff, concerned with rehabilitation (1992),
ISBN 92-871-1966-X, € 7,62 / US$ 12

The conceptual framework of the international classification of impairments; disabilities and handicaps (ICIDH) (1992),
ISBN 92-871-1972-4, € 7,62 / US$ 12

The use of the International classification of impairments, disabilities and handicaps (ICIDH) in mental health (1991),
ISBN 92-871-1939-2, € 10,67 / US$ 18

Evaluation of the use of the International classification of impairments, disabilities and handicaps (ICIDH) in surveys and health related statistics (1990),
ISBN 92-871-1852 3, € 7,62 / US$ 12

The use of the International classification of impairments, disabilities and handicaps (ICIDH) in rehabilitation (1989),
ISBN 92-871-1767-5, € 7,62 / US$ 12

Assessment of disabled people with a view to vocational rehabilitation measures, Strasbourg (1987)

Training of health care staff concerned with rehabilitation: present situation in member States and proposals for the improvement of such training (report P SG (84) 14)

Leisure, sports activities and holidays for disabled people (1982),
ISBN 92-871-0005-5

The functioning of sheltered workshops (1982),
ISBN 1982 92-871-0003-9

Information systems on impaired, disabled and handicapped people (1982),
ISBN 1982 92-871-0007-1

Adaptation of housing and surrounding areas to the needs of disabled persons (1979) (report P SG (79) 4)

Services for those disabled people who need special conditions of employment (1977) (report PA/SG (77) 19)

Identification of disabled persons (1977) (report PA/SG (77) 20)

Ways of facilitating access to and use of means of public transport by disabled people (1975) (report PA/SG (75) 11)

Rehabilitation of persons suffering from cerebral palsy (1973) (report PA/SG (73) 3)

Rehabilitation of hemiplegics (1972) (report PA/SG (72) 17)

Rehabilitation after myocardial infarction (1971) (report PA/SG (70) 33)

Early rehabilitation of persons suffering from chronic hepatic disorders (1971) (report PA/SG (70) 31)

Rehabilitation of cardiac cases (Bouillaud's disease) (1970) (report PA/SG (69) 25 revised)

Rehabilitation of persons suffering from ankylosing spondylitis (1967) (report PA/SG (67) 20)

Rehabilitation of those suffering from hearing and speech defects (1967) (report PA/SG (67) 21

The supply of prostheses (1967) (report PA/SG (67) 24)

III. Other relevant treaties, Recommendations, Resolutions and Publications of the Council of Europe

1. European Treaties

Convention for the Protection of Human Rights and Fundamental Freedoms (1950), ETS 005

European Convention on Social and Medical Assistance (1953), ETS 014

European Social Charter (1961), ETS 035

European Code of Social Security (1964), ETS 048

European Convention on Social Security (1972), ETS 078

European Convention for the Prevention of Torture and Inhuman or Degrading Treatment or Punishment (1987), ETS 126

European Code of Social Security (Revised) (1990), ETS 139

European Social Charter (revised)(1996), ETS 163

Convention for the protection of Human Rights and dignity of the human being with regard to the application of biology and medicine: Convention on Human Rights and Biomedecine (1997), ETS 164

2. Committee of Ministers

Recommendation (2004) 10 on the protection of the human rights and dignity of persons with mental disorder

Recommendation (2003) 19 on improving access to social rights

Recommendation (2002) 8 on child day-care

Recommendation (2002) 5 on the protection of women against violence

Recommendation (2001) 19 (Member states) on the participation of citizens in local public life

Recommendation (2001) 12 on the adaptation of health care services to the demand for health care and health care services of people in marginal situations

Recommendation (2001) 1 on social workers

Recommendation (2000) 18 on criteria for the development of health promotion policies

Recommendation (2000) 5 on the development of structures for citizen and patient participation in the decision-making process affecting health care

Recommendation (99) 17 on the improvement of co-operation among member States in the social security field

Recommendation (99) 14 on universal community service concerning new communication and information services

Recommendation (99) 9 on the role of sport in furthering social cohesion

Recommendation (99) 4 on principles concerning the legal protection of incapable adults

Recommendation (99) 2 on secondary education

Recommendation (98) 11 on the organisation of health care services for the chronically ill

Recommendation (98) 9 on dependence

Recommendation (98) 3 on access to higher education

Recommendation (97) 8 on rehabilitation through sport of people with disabilities in Bosnia and Herzegovina

Recommendation (96) 5 on reconciling work and family life

Recommendation (90) 22 on the protection of mental health of certain vulnerable groups in society

Recommendation (86) 18 on the European Charter on Sport for All: Disabled persons

3. Parliamentary Assembly

Recommendation 1592 (2003) Towards full social inclusion of people with disabilities

Recommendation 1562 (2002) Controlling the diagnosis and treatment of hyperactive children in Europe

Recommendation 1560 (2002) Towards concerted efforts for treating and curing spinal cord injury

Recommendation 1235 (1994) on psychiatry and human rights

Recommendation 1185 (1992) on rehabilitation policies for the disabled

4. Congress of Local and Regional Authorities of Europe

Resolution 216 (1990) on the rehabilitation of the disabled: role of local authorities

5. Publications

Access to social rights in Europe (2002),
ISBN 92-871-4984-4 , € 15 / US$ 23

Improving the quality of life of elderly persons in situations of dependency (2002), ISBN 92-871-5000-1

Strategy for Social Cohesion, CDCS (2000) 43

Opportunity and risk: Trends of social exclusion in Europe (1998), HDSE (98/1)

Action plan for Bosnia and Herzegovina: "Rehabilitation through sport" (1996)

Employment strategies for people with disabilities: the role of employers (1995), ISBN 92-871-2889-8, € 7,62 / US$ 12

Report on the integration of disabled children into their family and society (1989), ISBN 92-871-1756-X

Social policy and reintegration of handicapped children suffering from cancer (1986), ISBN 92-871-0916-8

Sales agents for publications of the Council of Europe
Agents de vente des publications du Conseil de l'Europe

BELGIUM/BELGIQUE
La Librairie européenne SA
50, avenue A. Jonnart
B-1200 BRUXELLES 20
Tel.: (32) 2 734 0281
Fax: (32) 2 735 0860
E-mail: info@libeurop.be
http://www.libeurop.be

Jean de Lannoy
202, avenue du Roi
B-1190 BRUXELLES
Tel.: (32) 2 538 4308
Fax: (32) 2 538 0841
E-mail: jean.de.lannoy@euronet.be
http://www.jean-de-lannoy.be

CANADA
Renouf Publishing Company Limited
5369 Chemin Canotek Road
CDN-OTTAWA, Ontario, K1J 9J3
Tel.: (1) 613 745 2665
Fax: (1) 613 745 7660
E-mail: order.dept@renoufbooks.com
http://www.renoufbooks.com

CZECH REPUBLIC/
RÉPUBLIQUE TCHÈQUE
Suweco Cz Dovoz Tisku Praha
Ceskomoravska 21
CZ-18021 PRAHA 9
Tel.: (420) 2 660 35 364
Fax: (420) 2 683 30 42
E-mail: import@suweco.cz

DENMARK/DANEMARK
GAD Direct
Fiolstaede 31-33
DK-1171 COPENHAGEN K
Tel.: (45) 33 13 72 33
Fax: (45) 33 12 54 94
E-mail: info@gaddirect.dk

FINLAND/FINLANDE
Akateeminen Kirjakauppa
Keskuskatu 1, PO Box 218
FIN-00381 HELSINKI
Tel.: (358) 9 121 41
Fax: (358) 9 121 4450
E-mail: akatilaus@stockmann.fi
http://www.akatilaus.akateeminen.com

FRANCE
La Documentation française
(Diffusion/Vente France entière)
124, rue H. Barbusse
F-93308 AUBERVILLIERS Cedex
Tel.: (33) 01 40 15 70 00
Fax: (33) 01 40 15 68 00
E-mail: commandes.vel@ladocfrancaise.gouv.fr
http://www.ladocfrancaise.gouv.fr

Librairie Kléber (Vente Strasbourg)
Palais de l'Europe
F-67075 STRASBOURG Cedex
Fax: (33) 03 88 52 91 21
E-mail: librairie.kleber@coe.int

GERMANY/ALLEMAGNE
AUSTRIA/AUTRICHE
August Bebel Allee 6
Am Hofgarten 10
D-53175 BONN
Tel.: (49) 2 28 94 90 20
Fax: (49) 2 28 94 90 222
E-mail: bestellung@uno-verlag.de
http://www.uno-verlag.de

GREECE/GRÈCE
Librairie Kauffmann
28, rue Stadiou
GR-ATHINAI 10564
Tel.: (30) 1 32 22 160
Fax: (30) 1 32 30 320
E-mail: ord@otenet.gr

HUNGARY/HONGRIE
Euro Info Service
Hungexpo Europa Kozpont ter 1
H-1101 BUDAPEST
Tel.: (361) 264 8270
Fax: (361) 264 8271
E-mail: euroinfo@euroinfo.hu
http://www.euroinfo.hu

ITALY/ITALIE
Libreria Commissionaria Sansoni
Via Duca di Calabria 1/1, CP 552
I-50125 FIRENZE
Tel.: (39) 556 4831
Fax: (39) 556 41257
E-mail: licosa@licosa.com
http://www.licosa.com

NETHERLANDS/PAYS-BAS
De Lindeboom Internationale Publikaties
PO Box 202, MA de Ruyterstraat 20 A
NL-7480 AE HAAKSBERGEN
Tel.: (31) 53 574 0004
Fax: (31) 53 572 9296
E-mail: books@delindeboom.com
Http://www.delindeboom.com

NORWAY/NORVÈGE
Akademika, A/S Universitetsbokhandel
PO Box 84, Blindern
N-0314 OSLO
Tel.: (47) 22 85 30 30
Fax: (47) 23 12 24 20

POLAND/POLOGNE
Główna Księgarnia Naukowa
im. B. Prusa
Krakowskie Przedmiescie 7
PL-00-068 WARSZAWA
Tel.: (48) 29 22 66
Fax: (48) 22 26 64 49
E-mail: inter@internews.com.pl
http://www.internews.com.pl

PORTUGAL
Livraria Portugal
Rua do Carmo, 70
P-1200 LISBOA
Tel.: (351) 13 47 49 82
Fax: (351) 13 47 02 64
E-mail: liv.portugal@mail.telepac.pt

SPAIN/ESPAGNE
Mundi-Prensa Libros SA
Castelló 37
E-28001 MADRID
Tel.: (34) 914 36 37 00
Fax: (34) 915 75 39 98
E-mail: libreria@mundiprensa.es
http://www.mundiprensa.com

SWITZERLAND/SUISSE
Adeco – Van Diermen
Chemin du Lacuez 41
CH-1807 BLONAY
Tel.: (41) 21 943 26 73
Fax: (41) 21 943 36 05
E-mail: info@adeco.org

UNITED KINGDOM/ROYAUME-UNI
TSO (formerly HMSO)
51 Nine Elms Lane
GB-LONDON SW8 5DR
Tel.: (44) 207 873 8372
Fax: (44) 207 873 8200
E-mail: customer.services@theso.co.uk
http://www.the-stationery-office.co.uk
http://www.itsofficial.net

UNITED STATES and CANADA/
ÉTATS-UNIS et CANADA
Manhattan Publishing Company
2036 Albany Post Road
CROTON-ON-HUDSON,
NY 10520, USA
Tel.: (1) 914 271 5194
Fax: (1) 914 271 5856
E-mail: Info@manhattanpublishing.com
http://www.manhattanpublishing.com

Council of Europe Publishing/Editions du Conseil de l'Europe
F-67075 Strasbourg Cedex
Tel.: (33) 03 88 41 25 81 – Fax: (33) 03 88 41 39 10 – E-mail: publishing@coe.int – Website: http://book.coe.int